THE ADIRONDACKS

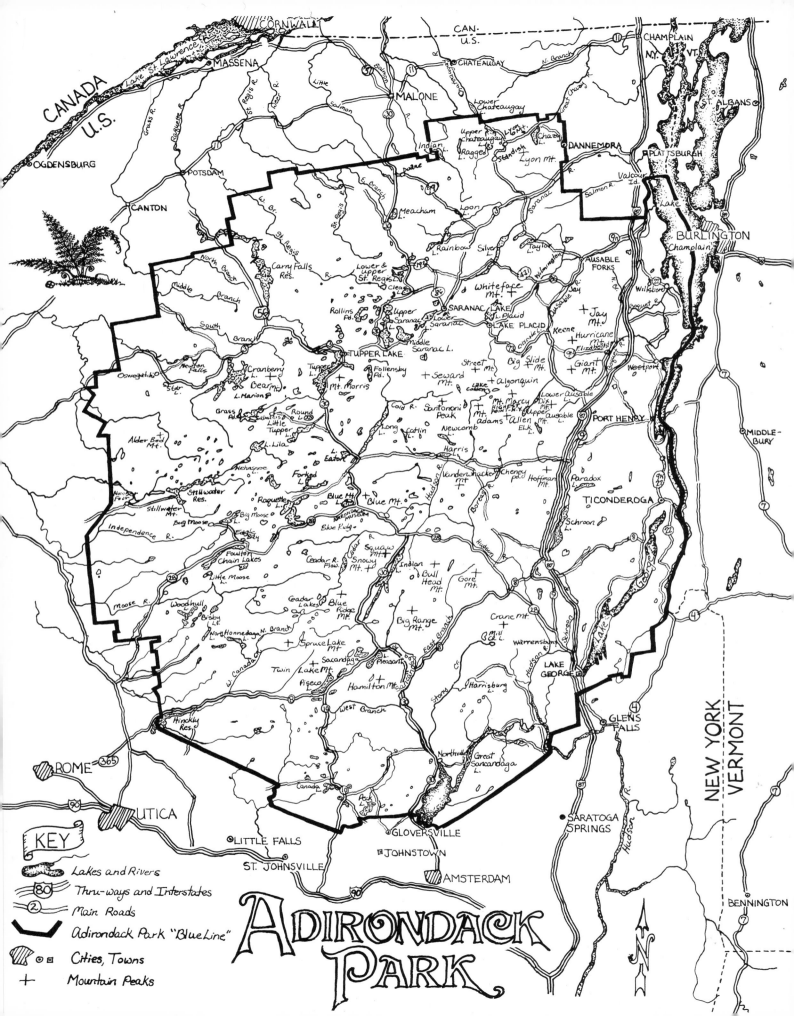

THE ADIRONDACKS

Clyde H. Smith

Introduction
by Lionel A. Atwill

A Studio Book   THE VIKING PRESS   New York

First published in 1976 by The Viking Press
625 Madison Avenue, New York, N.Y. 10022

Published simultaneously in Canada by
The Macmillan Company of Canada Limited

Text and black-and-white photographs printed in the
United States of America

Color photographs printed in Japan

Library of Congress Cataloging in Publication Data

Smith, Clyde H
The Adirondacks.
(A Studio book)
1. Adirondack Mountains—Description and travel.   2. Smith, Clyde H.   I. Title.
F127.A2S59   917.47′53′044   76-10687
ISBN 0-670-10481-7

Contents

To ELIZABETH
for inspiration, encouragement, and faith

Preface

It would take several lifetimes to explore the Adirondack region, and even then the surface would hardly be scratched. It is a spectacular land of mountains, lakes, rivers, waterfalls, wildlife, marshes, farmlands, and towns. In essence, the Adirondacks have just about everything except a seashore.

I have tried to portray the region's diversity through photography and accounts of related experiences; I have also tried to show a part of the Adirondacks that few people know or will ever see. This book is a result of love for the great Adirondack wild country and a desire to share with others a bit of its everlasting beauty.

Clyde H. Smith

MINK

Introduction

The Spirit of the Great North Woods
An Examination of the Character of the Adirondacks
by *Lionel A. Atwill*

The Adirondacks are complex, and the longer I live here, the more difficulty I have in describing their essence. At first textbook descriptions sufficed: six millon acres in northern New York; the largest wilderness in the East; the greatest park in the United States (larger, in fact, than Grand Canyon, Yellowstone, Yosemite, Olympic, and Glacier national parks combined); the land north of New York's Mohawk Valley and south of the Canadian border.

I soon discovered, however, that these phrases merely defined an area on a map. A tremendous void in the description of the Adirondacks was still missing. As I began to explore these millions of acres of woods, these thousands of miles of rivers and rushing streams, I found that there was a pulse to this land, a throb of power and majesty that coursed through these rivers, blew across the summits of the mountains, and even sounded in the deathly silence of a midnight snowstorm. The void in my description took form: it was the soul of the Adirondacks, the character of the wilderness, the spirit of the Great North Woods that was missing.

But how does one describe character—especially the character of land? It is a subjective quality that is sensed rather than seen. Photographs, especially photographs by a sensitive man like Clyde Smith, are perhaps most effective. They capture, in part, some of the moods of the Adirondacks, some of the pulse of the land. The writer is left with facts, history, experiences, and interpretation. He cannot say to the reader, "Look! There it is—see for yourself." He forces the reader to see through his eyes and feel through his emotions. I hope, however, that I can strike a few chords of harmony with these superb photographs in portraying the character of the Adirondacks.

A scant mile west of the upper reaches of the Oswegatchie River on a razorback ridge overlooking ponds on both sides is a stand of pines that has never felt the bite of the woodsman's ax or heard the staccato whine of a chain saw. The trunks are straight and tall, towering eighty to a hundred feet above the forest's floor. A dense canopy sifts the sun's rays, and only where one of the giants has fallen can an unbroken beam of light knife through.

It is seven-thirty in the morning, and as I sit on a decaying log in the midst of these woods, listening to the early-morning bustle of forest life—chipmunks flitting through the duff and making far too much noise for their size, the rasp of branches rubbing in the wind, and the crescendo cry of a solitary loon on the pond below—I feel a tremendous sense of exclusivity, as if these woods were mine and mine alone.

Because of the coverage of the trees, little grows on the forest's floor, and one can walk between these giants with relative ease. Still, the climb here has taken me almost an hour from my campsite on the Oswegatchie, but I'm a confirmed dawdler and can rarely walk through any stretch of woods without stopping periodically to examine a delicate mushroom or whack a hollow tree in the hope that an owl or raccoon might appear. Fortunately, though, I have no appointment to keep on this spot. I have come here, by car, canoe, and now on foot, only to enjoy these surroundings and to absorb a few sensory pleasures that I can call my own.

Sensory pleasures draw many people to the Adirondacks, because this land is so drenched in spectacle and so willing to share its beauty with visitors in a very personal way. If one climbs Algonquin Peak or Mount Marcy in the dead of winter or takes a hike for the day to a remote pond named Ox Shoe, Grizzle Ocean, Artist, or Slim, then one doesn't need postcards to recall the sights and sounds along the way. "Our campaign in the Adirondacks seems almost like a dream; it has idealized itself already, and my life will always be the sweeter and richer for it. How it enhances the value of living, does it not? to have something sweet to remember!" wrote John Burroughs, the turn-of-the-century naturalist, after a trip to the Adirondacks.

There is something in the Adirondacks that fulfills this need for "something sweet to remember" more fully than many other wilderness areas I have known. It is, perhaps, its ability to give visitors that important sense of exclusivity that I felt on my log near the Oswegatchie—like a gracious host who can make every guest feel like the center of attention. Ask any two people what the Adirondacks are, and they will tell you *their* unique experience that to them symbolizes the Adirondacks.

"Why, I had that trout hooked solid as could be, and then, by God, it took a turn around the pool, and the next thing I knew I was reeling in air."

"We'd gone all the way through Harris Riff below Blue Ledge with no more than a gallon of water in the canoe, when my bow man turns around to see where we'd been, and we hit a boulder about the size of the *Queen Mary*. It took us two hours to peel the canoe off that rock."

Fishermen, hunters, hikers, canoeists, and the other wilderness travelers who expore the inner Adirondacks have shared in experiences that are unique, and those sensory pleasures are a small part of the Adirondacks that they will carry with them forever.

But what is the Adirondacks' secret? How does it combine this sense of dignity and congeniality that makes people talk of "my" Adirondacks, as if they shared secrets with the land, and return year after year to "their" Adirondacks, as if the trip were a divine pilgrimage? Why do people stand in awe of the Adirondacks? I can only speculate and carry the comparison to the perfect host one step further: his ability is credited to maturity, worldliness, and wisdom, and I suppose that the same traits could be applied to the Adirondacks.

Certainly these mountains, forests, lakes, and streams are mature. Geologists view certain rock formations in the Adirondacks as some of the oldest in the world, dating back possibly three billion years. At one time the mountains of the Adirondacks exceeded 20,000 feet in height, yet today the highest mountain in the Adirondacks and in New York State, Mount Marcy, is only 5344 feet above sea level, eroded through the centuries by glaciers, wind, and rain.

Maturity does not necessarily accompany old age, however; it requires continual change in response to external conditions, and certainly the Adirondacks have changed and continue to do so. The most recent face-lifting occurred almost a million years ago during the Pleistocene epoch, when massive glaciers swept down from the north, grinding down the mountains, gouging out lakes and rivers, and depositing vast quantities of soil from Canada throughout the valleys. When the Ice Age ended some ten thousand years ago, the countenance of the Adirondacks had undergone a major change.

More than two thousand lakes and ponds were formed, some no larger than Lake Tear of the Clouds, a shimmering pond high on the shoulder of Mount Marcy from which trickles a stream that eventually increases in power to form the source of the mighty Hudson River. Other lakes, such as Saranac, Placid, George, Long, Tupper, Raquette, Indian, and Schroon, are massive bodies of waters capable of catering to the needs of water skiers, sailors, boating enthusiasts, and the solitary fisherman.

The glaciers formed two major drainage basins for the more than 100,000 miles of flowing waterways. To the east, north, and west, rivers lead to the St. Lawrence, while the Hudson carries off water to the south. The Hudson of the Adirondacks and the Hudson that sludges past the docks of New York City are the same river in little more than name. The northern Hudson is a free-flowing, cold, clear mountain river that in its travels from the side of Mount Marcy passes through some of the most spectacular scenery in the Adirondacks and offers perhaps the most challenging white water canoeing in the East.

Along with Mount Marcy stand over a hundred mountains of 3400 feet or more clustered primarily in five north-south oriented ranges on the eastern edge of the central Adirondacks. More than forty of these giants tower above 4000 feet, and although their rounded profiles and weathered

12

slopes give them the appearance of hills from a distance, at closer range their massiveness becomes readily apparent. They are scarred by blowdowns, slides, and fires, and often their summits are barren; but in a solid, permanent sort of way they are extremely beautiful. They don't flaunt their beauty like the younger mountains of the west; instead, their grace is revealed in subtle shades—the play of light across their sides, the careful blend of hardwoods and evergreens peaking to a summit of dark gray rock, and the clouds, drifting like veils between their peaks.

The Adirondacks are still changing. Every year numerous minor earthquakes are reported, and although few can be felt and the greatest damage is usually a broken teacup, these quakes do indicate a state of constant change in the land.

Wisdom and worldliness are perhaps more difficult terms to associate with a geographic area than maturity, but if one considers the history that the Adirondacks has seen pass before them, then one must grant them a modicum of intelligence, and if worldliness can be equated to exposure to a variety of cultures, then the Adirondacks certainly qualify.

The Iroquois and Algonquins were probably the first men to walk through this wilderness. These two warring tribes never lived in the heart of the Adirondacks (although there were scattered settlements in peripheral areas), because the winters were just too hostile for survival, but they did hunt and fish throughout the woods, and both tribes viewed several areas in the Adirondacks as sacred territories that enjoyed a neutral status.

Their legacy still remains in the Indian names that are found throughout the Adirondacks, although many of these titles sprang from the fertile minds of nineteenth-century tourist promoters, who felt that such names lent an air of mystery to the North Woods. Even the name Adirondack sings with the sound of war parties and stalking braves, but it was actually applied to the area by Ebenezer Emmons, a geologist and surveyor, in 1838. Local legend views the name as a bastardization of a derogatory Iroquois phrase *ratirontaks*, meaning "those who eat trees," which was used in reference to the Algonquin, who, when times were hard, reportedly ate bark.

13

The first white settlers came to the area in the eighteenth century, building homes and clearing fields mostly along the fertile Champlain Valley. During the Revolutionary War this part of the Adirondacks played a most important role. Fort Ticonderoga, Crown Point, Lake George, and Lake Champlain are names familiar to all students of history, and today a careful search of the shoreline of either Lake George or Lake Champlain can turn up musket and cannon balls.

A few hardy pioneers ventured inland after the Revolution, but it was not until the years between 1850 and 1900 that the Adirondacks enjoyed their greatest growth. The woods were promoted as an unspoiled wilderness, overflowing with game and fish, and Eastern society began to arrive by carriage and boat and private railroad car to reap these spoils. At the same time the logging and mining industries found untapped riches in the woods. More than two hundred iron mines were worked in the Adirondacks, and although few produced high-grade ore, several were notable exceptions. At Mineville, on the eastern edge of the Adirondacks, the iron for the Civil War vessel *Monitor* was reputedly mined, and at the MacIntyre works in the interior of the Adirondacks vast quantities of ore were removed until a large concentration of supposedly useless impurities forced the closing of the mine. Those impurities were later discovered to be titanium, and today NL Industries operates a vast titanium mine in the same area.

Perhaps more impressive than a history of the land is an account of the people who have lived and visited here. Shortly after the battle of Waterloo Napoleon's brother, Joseph, the deposed king of Spain, purchased more than 150,000 acres on the western edge of the Adirondacks for less than one dollar per acre. If his brother could escape from captivity, they would flee to the Adirondacks to establish a new empire, a new France. The plan never materialized, of course, but today there is a Lake Bonaparte in the Adirondacks.

John Brown was a struggling farmer on the outskirts of Lake Placid before he took up his banner of abolition and met his death at Harpers Ferry. Now he rests near his reconstructed farm in the shadows of Mount Marcy and the High Peaks.

From the 1850s on, a series of luminaries visited and lived in the Adirondacks: Rockefellers, Vanderbilts, Whitneys, Morgans, and Mellons, Robert Louis Stevenson, Mark Twain, Ned Buntline, and Sigmund Freud —the list goes on to include philosophers and philanderers, kings and presidents. They came to the Adirondacks, for the most part, to enjoy the sporting life of the Great North Woods. John Burroughs, who was so memorably affected by his first trip to the Adirondacks, took a subsequent motor tour through the woods in the company of Henry Ford, Thomas Edison, and Harvey Firestone. Burroughs supplied the insight, Ford the autos, Edison the portable lighting system for the camp, and Firestone presumably donated a few spare tires. And it was on the side of Mount Marcy that Teddy Roosevelt was informed of McKinley's death and his new status as the twenty-sixth President of the United States.

Eighty miles southeast of the headquarters of the Oswegatchie on the eastern shore of Lake George is the greatest freshwater wetland in New York State. Dunham, Harris, and Warner bays cover a thousand acres with marsh grasses, cattails, pond lilies, and duckweed, and their twisting networks of streams and fertile bogs provide an ideal habitat for countless species of wildlife.

In the spring, northern pike, rainbow trout, bullhead, perch, sunfish, and bass invade the shallows to stake out spawning beds. Within the grass and along the shoreline nest herons, woodpeckers, jays, hawks, and a variety of waterfowl, while beavers, muskrats, otters, minks, and raccoons prowl along the banks. This marsh is as much a part of the Adirondacks as the stand of virgin pine near the Oswegatchie, yet the two areas are radically different in their physical characteristics.

It is precisely this diversity that adds another dimension to the character of the Adirondacks. Nothing can be taken for granted; there are always surprises around the corner; and what may appear at first to be the obvious may prove to be rather complex and incongruous. For example, the delineation of "The Adirondacks." The Adirondack Park is a six-million-acre amalgam of State-owned and privately owned land. It is delineated by a line encompassing most of the land north of the Mohawk Valley, south of the Canadian border, west of the Champlain Valley, and east of the St. Lawrence River. This line defines the largest park of any kind in the United States, an area roughly the size of neighboring Vermont.

Of the six million acres, roughly 2.3 million are owned by the State of New York and are known as the Adirondack Forest Preserve, an area that "shall remain forever as wild forest land" under Article XIV of the New York State Constitution. When this "Forever Wild" act was conceived in 1894, the State envisioned one day owning all of the land within the mapped outline. Total State ownership never became a reality, however, and so today there exists a very complex checkerboard of State-owned and privately owned land. Fortunately, the physical characteristics of the Forest Preserve and a great deal of privately owned land are the same, so there is a cohesiveness, at least in appearance, to the Park. In an effort to preserve the integrity of the Park, the Adirondack Park Agency was formed in the latter part of 1971. The Park Agency is charged with controlling the development of both State-owned and privately owned lands and insuring that the Adirondacks remain a cohesive entity.

While the land within this originally designated area is officially known as the Adirondacks, the sections that fall just outside of this political boundary cannot be neglected. Ask a resident of Hannawa Falls or Owl's Head (towns that are outside of the original boundary) where he or she lives, and the answer would most certainly be, "Why, in the Adirondacks, of course." It may all sound like an insignificant matter of semantics, but to an Adirondacker, a person from the North Country, a woodchuck (as we are sometimes affectionately called), it's a matter of pride.

Perhaps the best definition of the Adirondacks lies in the story of Sunday Rock, a large boulder near the road a few miles south of Colton. In the nineteenth century when travel into the Adirondacks was limited to a few dirt roads, this rock marked the northern entrance to the Adirondacks. After passing it, Sundays and all the other days of the week completely lost their meaning to the timelessness of the woods, and lumberjacks, trappers, sportsmen, and other adventurers no longer had to adhere to the conventions of civilization. And that, in spirit, is the Adirondacks.

The Oswegatchie and Dunham Bay are just two examples of the physical diversity of the Adirondacks. Better known and certainly more frequented are the High Peaks, the major mountains of the Adirondacks whose names ring with mystery: Santanoni, Wolf Jaw, Giant, Algonquin, Haystack, Sawteeth, Panther Peak, and Couchsachraga, to name a few. More than forty of these mountains crest above 4000 feet, and every year tens of thousands of climbers assault their summits. Most of the peaks are connected by trails maintained by either the Department of Environmental Conservation of the State of New York or private hiking clubs, such as the Adirondack Mountain Club. However, some of the mountains are still without trails, although excessive hiking pressure through the years has created numerous "herd paths," unofficial trails made by countless pairs of hiking boots all pointed in the same general direction.

Unfortunately, the High Peaks have been viewed as *the* major physical attraction of the Adirondacks ever since 1872, when Verplank Colvin embarked on a twenty-eight-year effort to survey the Adirondacks for the State. Verplank Colvin made a challenge out of the mountains. His measurements of their heights resulted in rankings and ultimately a made-to-measure checklist for the climber. Once some sort of order was established, people began climbing the mountains with a purpose: start with number one, Mount Marcy, and work through the list.

The fragile environment of the High Peaks has suffered from this traffic, especially at higher elevations where conditions are so delicate that a mere inch of soil might take hundreds of years to accumulate. Trails to the more popular peaks now resemble three-lane highways in spots, and on a major weekend in the middle of summer one can share the summit of a mountain with fifty or so other climbers. The damage that has been done can be prevented in the future by education (teaching people how and where to walk above timberline, for example) and by introducing Adirondack visitors to less publicized areas in the Park, such as the thousands of acres of lowland forest that blanket so much of the Adirondacks. These areas are perhaps less challenging to the peak-bagging purist, but they do offer a great deal of diversity in vegetation and wildlife.

In open contradiction to the wilderness of the High Peaks, the mystery of Dunham Bay, and the seclusion of the Oswegatchie is the rolling farmland that extends down the Champlain Valley and across the northern perimeter of the Park. Here the countryside resembles neighboring Vermont with cleared fields and stone fences. It is a rather dramatic sight to drive through this land in the early morning when the mist is rising from the fields and see cows and barns and an occasional farmer doing his morning chores and then, as the sun slowly burns off the haze, to see the grandeur of the wilderness materialize in the distance. It is a staggering contradiction, yet all a part of the Adirondacks.

A great variety of wildlife has called the Adirondacks home over the centuries. A hundred years ago mountain lions, timber wolves, elk, and moose roamed through the woods. As civilization descended on the Adirondacks, the extensive range needed by the timber wolf and mountain lion was sizably reduced, and both species were driven out of the Park. Just in the past few years, however, there have been numerous sightings reported of mountain lions in isolated pockets of the Adirondacks, and the possibility exists that a small number of cats, perhaps no more than two or three, have returned. Although the timber wolf will probably never return, there are eastern or brush wolves here today, as well as coyotes, whose eerie howls in the dead of night have driven more than one tenderfoot camper out of the woods.

The elk and moose population never was large, and early hunting pressure has always been credited with their demise. Recent investigations have proved this theory false, however. Both elk and moose succumbed to a parasite introduced to the Adirondacks by deer which moved into the wilderness on the heels of man.

Before extensive lumbering cleared much of the virgin growth of lumber and created thick new growths of brush and new trees, the whitetail deer could not find sufficient food in the heavily canopied climax forests to support them in large numbers. As man cleared these forests, however, the

18

deer entered in numbers, carrying with them a parasitic round worm, *Pneumistrongylus tenuis*, and a liver fluke, both of which had never before existed in the Adirondacks. Unfortunately, these two minuscule killers proved more harmful to the limited elk and moose population than all the hunters who preceded them, and in a short time after their arrival the elk and moose of the Adirondacks were just a memory.

Other species have disappeared from the Adirondacks: the peregrine falcon, wolverine, raven (although this species is trying for a comeback), lynx, and caribou, but the land is certainly not devoid of wildlife. In the High Peaks the whitetail population fluctuates due to heavy winter kills from extreme temperatures and blanketing snowstorms. The lower elevations can support good deer herds, however, and on some private estates where timber is harvested regularly and hunting is controlled, deer populations have grown to almost unmanageable sizes.

Black bear abound, although it is a rare sight to see one of these elusive animals in the woods. Before State laws closed the ever-present town dump in favor of strictly regulated sanitary landfills, it was not unusual to drive past a dump at night and mistake it for a drive-in movie. With headlights blazing, cars would park three and four deep to watch the bears on stage, rooting through the trash for an easy meal. Fortunately, this situation is pretty much in check in the Adirondacks today, and most bears have readjusted to eating in the wilds, although an occasional rogue will make a nuisance of himself at a popular campsite and will have to be tranquilized and carted off to a more suitable home.

Although heavy trapping pressure in the early part of this century almost destroyed the fur bearers in the Adirondacks, today, thanks to progressive game management, the Adirondacks abound in small game. Beaver colonies exist within a few hundred yards of the Adirondack Northway, the major artery into the Adirondacks, and it's not unusual to find at least one beaver lodge in every remote or semi-remote pond. Fisher, which were almost exterminated in the 1920s when their pelts brought up to eighty dollars apiece, are enjoying a strong comeback, and although they are rarely seen, the winter snow reveals their tracks, stalking, loping, and circling through the woods. Other elusive animals—bobcats, minks, river otters, and pine martens—roam the forests, and the thrill of seeing just one of these animals as it darts through the shadows or slinks along the bank of a stream is an unparalleled experience.

More than forty other mammals inhabit the Adirondacks, and many, such as the porcupine, skunk, and raccoon, make their presence all too well known to the unsuspecting woodsman. A patient observer can spot foxes, rabbits, woodchucks, chipmunks, muskrats, and, if he is lucky, a rare yellow-cheeked vole—an overgrown field mouse which is normally found in the northern reaches of Canada but which has set up a southern residence in the Adirondacks.

Only a few years ago several pairs of nesting bald eagles existed in the Adirondacks, fishing in the innumerable lakes and building their nests in towering pines and on craggy cliffs. But even in the wilds of the Adirondacks, the horrible effects of DDT and other insecticides have taken their toll. To sight an eagle is a rarity today, although in the spring and fall both golden and bald eagles use the Champlain Valley as a flyway and will occasionally venture inland. Mammal-eating raptors are more common than their fish-eating kin, and great horned owls, red-tailed hawks, and goshawks are frequently spotted circling high overhead.

Songbirds and game birds are plentiful, and the winter months are brightened by darting streaks of evening grosbeaks, blue jays, redpolls, and purple finches. In the High Peaks one can occasionally spot a ladder-backed three-toed woodpecker, a bird normally found in extreme northern climates.

Of all the birds in the Adirondacks, the loon is perhaps most symbolic of the mystery of the wilderness. Unable to walk on land without tripping over their clumsy rear-mounted webbed feet, loons are a thing of absolute beauty in the water, diving and gliding across the still surface of a fog-shrouded pond. But it is their cry—the cry of a wailing child, the cry of empty despair, a wavering, trilling crescendo that echoes across the water—that makes the loon the bird of the Adirondacks. To hear that sound in the early morning as the fog burns off the water and then to see the silhouette of the bird as it slowly drifts out of sight is the ultimate experience in the wilderness.

The 250,000 acres of lakes and ponds and the thousands of miles of streams and rivers in the Adirondacks yield many varieties of fish, from brook, brown, lake, and rainbow trout to bass, pike, perch, and panfish, and throughout the year, from trout season in the spring until ice fishing in the winter, thousands of anglers come to the Adirondacks to enjoy some of the finest fishing in the East.

The number of other cold-blooded animals in the Adirondacks is limited by the severe winter weather. Timber rattlers are occasionally seen near Lake George and north to Lake Champlain, but there has never been a reported snake-bite victim. At their most northern limit, just south of the village of Essex on Lake Champlain, the snakes congregate to spend the winter balled up in great clumps wedged in cracks and crannies in the rock. The unfortunate snakes nearest the entrance will freeze to death, but their bodies will preserve their companions from a similar fate. It is all part of survival in the Adirondacks.

The diversity of the Adirondacks is everywhere, and this spectrum of experience is a great part of the spirit of the Great North Woods. There is always adventure around the corner and mystery in the air.

For all the beauty, diversity, dignity, and congeniality of the area, the Adirondacks can be one of the most hostile places on earth. Because most people visit this land during periods of relative tranquillity, however, they are not aware of this side of the Adirondacks' character. Seasoned wilderness travelers have a very healthy respect for the devastating power that the Adirondacks can muster, a power that adds a final dimension to the character of this region.

When spring comes to the Adirondacks, it does not tread lightly. There is no gradual awakening, no slow blooming and unfurling of greens. Spring comes in one day, the day that the ice goes out and peacefully frozen streams are transformed into rushing torrents of frigid water.

Summer days and warm weather bring a sense of calm to the Adirondacks, but dangers still lurk in the wilderness. Thousands of hikers and campers set off into the mountains daily, and many are ill-prepared and ill-equipped for their journeys. Venturing out without map, compass, adequate food, and shelter, the unsuspecting will approach a trip through the interior of the Adirondacks as though it were a Sunday drive: just follow the signs down the wide-open trail, climb to the top of a mere 4000-foot hill, enjoy the view, and return home in time to watch the evening news.

Few make such a mistake more than once. The trail that may look like a garden path at its start can turn into an exhausting scramble across steeply pitched ledges and through dense underbrush. Roots and rocks grab and bruise feet at every step, mud clings like lead weights to pants and boots. Every ten-foot elevation change feels like a major assault. On less-traveled paths the actual route can mysteriously disappear, and the hiker can find himself hopelessly lost, caught in a tangle of brush and surrounded on four sides by solid walls of blowdown.

And although these mountains may not crest higher than 5000 feet, the approach to many of them may start far below 1000, so the climber must make a vertical ascent of several thousand feet over a route perhaps ten miles long. If one starts out on a bright, sunny day, there is no guarantee that the weather will not change radically within a few hours. Almost every summer snow falls periodically at higher elevations, and once the sun drops, temperatures generally plunge to 40 or 30 degrees and winds pick up to a steady howl. Even a shower can be dangerous. On June 29, 1963, six inches of rain fell on the summit of Giant Mountain within ninety minutes, uprooting trees and causing massive landslides that cut twenty- and thirty-foot swatches through the woods.

Fall and winter in the Adirondacks pose even greater threats. The weather conditions on the top of the mountains are severe, with winds of more than a hundred miles an hour and temperatures far below zero. Snowstorms can cause complete white-outs, erasing all signs of trails and limiting visibility to no more than a few feet. Even during relatively clear weather the ever-present cold can destroy. In 1974 two hikers set out over the Thanksgiving weekend on a relatively easy trip during average climatic conditions. Thirty hours later one of the hikers, a twenty-three-year-old, was dead of exposure. The power of the Adirondacks is absolute and a character trait not to be taken lightly.

Everyone has his own Adirondacks. Mine is the dignity and congeniality of the Oswegatchie, the diversity of Dunham Bay. I can see and smell and sense these areas in my mind, and they shall always signify the spirit of the Adirondacks to me.

But my Adirondacks are a very biased, personal representation of this region, a picture that springs from my own vision and is reflected and warped by my interpretation of the character of this land. A clearer picture comes through the lens of a camera, and no one whom I know is more adept at capturing that image than Clyde Smith. He is a fellow traveler through the wilderness, a great friend, and a man who knows the essence of the Adirondacks. If John Burroughs were alive today, I am sure that he would agree that such photography captures, at least in part, the mystical quality of the Adirondacks that gives those of us who know and love the region "something sweet to remember."

White-Water Wilderness

With a cupped hand I reach over the side of my canoe and scoop up a palmful of clear water. It is clean, refreshing, and potable . . . it is the Hudson.

To drink directly from the Hudson is unbelievable. If you were to examine the river as it flows through New York City, or up along its familiar route past Poughkeepsie, Kingston, Albany, and on to Glens Falls, the thought would be repulsive. Like so many large rivers in our country today, the Hudson is saturated with industrial pollution through much of its length.

But if you trace its course farther north into the Adirondack Forest Preserve where the young river squeezes through deep gorges and around enormous boulders, you will find drinkable water. You will also find a country of unparalleled beauty. Here the Hudson lives, breathes—and surges unmolested. For nearly thirty miles no roads and few trails penetrate the Hudson's wild plunge from Newcomb to the tiny village of North River. Its gradient sometimes drops at the rate of 100 feet per mile—a supreme challenge for white-water canoeists, demanding every ounce of skill and experience. Mangled remains of shattered canoes along the way attest to the river's ruthless power. An unfortunate adventurer who overestimates his ability may end up losing craft and gear, and then spend several days extracting himself from the Hudson Gorge on foot.

In the shadow of this risk I have returned to the upper Hudson time and again to absorb its spectacular setting and enjoy the thrill of running its rapids. It is a wilderness of solitude and intrigue—filled with interlacing side streams, thundering waterfalls, and corrugated ravines, and sprinkled with a multitude of ponds and lakes.

And now, as our canoes glide over a smooth black lagoon after launching at Newcomb, the anticipation of what lies ahead sends a shiver

24

of excitement through my body. Our party consists of three boat crews—all Hudson veterans and each with his own desire to revisit a part of the Adirondack wilderness few people ever dare to venture into. A steady cadence of water dripping from our paddles is the only sound that breaks the ominous silence. Curious wisps of mist cling to the water's surface and part like transparent veils as our canoes knife along on this mottled sea of mystery.

Ahead, the shores of thick cedars and tall pines merge to a tiny notch—it seems the river must end abruptly. A faint muffled growl drifts up from the cleft, and with each stroke of our paddles its volume increases until at last, as we round a bend, there is no mistake about the noise—tossing white spouts are leaping across the river's width. It is the first big rapid. Beyond, a void—the waters drop, how steeply we do not know, for it's difficult to determine from our position close to the river's surface.

Within minutes the river has become a swiftly moving conveyor belt propelling us at breakneck speed toward the brink. Frantically we search the shores for a place to land our canoes. Pivoting upstream, we struggle against the current and stroke toward a spot just above the turmoil.

Upon landing, we dash across slippery rocks to examine the torrent thundering down a natural staircase and disappearing in a cloud of vapor. It is like looking into a vortex of time, recalling the colorful drama of log drives of the past. The last logs were floated downriver in 1950, but before that, for a hundred years, the mighty Hudson served as a vital artery for logging operations.

Scrambling along the ledges, we plot a course for our canoes through the complex wave formations. We will run the rapids one canoe at a time— that way, if an upset should occur, those on shore may be able to assist the swamped party. However, on a big river there is little that can be done to aid a dumped canoe. Because of the swiftly moving current, about all the canoeists can manage to do is stick with their craft until they are swept to a calm pool or are able to navigate toward a bank.

The first canoe enters the sluice and is sucked toward the big haystacks like a bobbing cork. Deliberately the canoeists backpaddle to check their forward momentum and prevent larger waves from filling their boat.

Stroking quickly, they twist and drop around partially submerged boulders, then shoot back into the swirling passage that leads over a breath-taking stairway of foaming water to a pool far below.

Now it is our turn. We push off and are immediately drawn like a magnet toward the gushing caldron. Our canoe bounces over the waves and plunges into booming holes, then pops out again, spewing foam and spray. The sound of crashing water is deafening as it reverberates off the chasm walls. One moment we seem suspended in air, the next engulfed in a torrential immersion. Twisting and turning, we thread our way around monstrous boulders, past boiling whirlpools, and back into the corkscrew of thrashing waves. In one final surge we are projected out on a pool of eerie mist. Our boat is full to the gunwales, but miraculously we still float.

Gingerly we maneuver our nearly sunken craft toward shore. The bottom rotates, and we splash wildly with our paddles to retain its balance. Our companions reach out to steady us and we land. Suddenly the third boat shoots out from the swirling mist, riding very low. We all cheer, and helping hands stretch out to assist its occupants too. Many gallons of Hudson water are dumped back into the river—then we stand around with silly grins on our faces, looking with awe at the pounding cascade that has just delivered us to the threshold of white-water adventure.

There is a new spirit now, one of confidence but not without caution. Having successfully negotiated the first tricky rapids, we look ahead—the river beckons and we launch again.

Soon we enter a picturesque valley crowded with dense stands of pines and cedars. There are short runs of manageable rapids which seem tame compared to our initial plunge. These are spliced with long sections of flat water in between as the Hudson flows directly south for about ten miles. Then the river bed gets steeper and the valley narrows. From a rocky gorge beside a small mountain, Cedar River gushes and merges with the Hudson in a foaming tempest that is the beginning of a long series of continuous rapids. We paddle like demons toward shore and land on a hemlock-crowned point. The thrashing rapids are impossible to reconnoiter because they disappear beyond our line of sight downriver. We will have to make on-the-spot decisions, so, with pounding excitement, we push off.

26

Within seconds the river's powerful current draws us toward enormous standing waves. If we try bashing through them, we will surely swamp, but by backpaddling at just the right moment we can slow our headlong momentum and ride the crests without taking on water. So now turbulence that caused us to gasp earlier becomes an exhilarating roller coaster drawing us ever onward toward the Hudson's throbbing heart. We fairly dance along the next few miles, whooping and cheering.

Then the Hudson, which has been flowing in a straight southerly direction, makes an abrupt turn east. Here the Indian River converges with it, revitalizing the main stream, which then plunges into a magnificent canyon of sculptured rock studded with cedar thickets. Within the confines of towering walls the roar of the rapids is accentuated, and we guide our canoes in a zigzag course down its rocky throat. Dark holes and water-worn chambers mark the cliffs on each side. In another few miles the north wall recedes and a dashing tributary gushes from an enchanting glen. It is called Mink Pond Brook and originates at a cluster of ponds a mile or so above the main gorge.

We decide to beach our canoes and investigate. Through a haze of early spring leaves I can see flashing water spill over a wall about a hundred feet back from the Hudson. We scramble over moss-covered rocks beside the crystal stream cascading down its velvety green carpet. Ferns and wildflowers dripping with moisture sway in air currents wafting from the waterfall's grotto. Everything is saturated with dewy droplets that shimmer and glisten in shafts of late-afternoon sunlight.

Suddenly two deer, unaware of our presence in the waterfall's din, bolt past us with high-flung white tails. I stand there with my mouth open and my camera at my side—the fleeting moment has slipped by and only a memory has been recorded.

We wonder about making our campsite here, but somehow it seems too sacred a place, so we launch once again into the Hudson. The river begins a twisting course, the canyon walls soar taller, and the rapids increase in severity as the drops get progressively steeper. We enter some heavy waves, then a jumble of monstrous boulders that hug a large, sweeping curve. Pulling around the turn, I look down a long series of incredibly difficult drops—nearly a half mile of torturous waves and deep souse holes. There is no time to head for shore, and even if we could, there would be no place to land along the rocky walls. Our companions are skittering along the river's edge, pirouetting from boulder to boulder, but we are too far to the center. No amount of backpaddling can check our speed, and we crash with shuddering impact into the mountain of waves.

A stiff wind blows upriver, spraying the tops off whitecaps. There is backlighting on the crests—how I wish for a moment to snap a photo, but there's not a second to spare. Every reflex must concentrate on keeping our craft in a straight line. Our canoe is half full of water, and a broadside now would surely finish us. Thundering holes boil all around, and we dive . . . the bow disappears . . . then pops to the surface. We are nearly full of water but still going straight. Then I look up and for the first time am aware of a giant monolith rising from the river before us, a towering wall of rock nearly eight hundred feet high—it is Blue Ledge. A deep green pool laps at its base, and for a moment there is hope that we might reach the calm water without tipping over.

But at the same instant that my eyes have taken in the scene, we dive again into a sucking souse hole that stands our canoe on end. In a wild frenzy of foam we catapult from our boat and are swimming the last few yards toward Blue Ledge pool. Our canoe ejects from the hole and wallows nearby. We grab its trailing stern line and tow it toward shore. Fortunately all our gear is in waterproof bags and tied securely inside the canoe.

We drag ourselves out of the water like a couple of bedraggled muskrats. Our comrades paddle in with boats awash. Somehow they managed to thread a route closer to shore and avoid the bigger drops. We regard our dumping as an important lesson in humility—before entering Blue Ledge rapids, we had an air of cockiness because we had successfully stayed afloat thus far. Nothing humbles "experts" quicker than floating by their friends upside down!

A rocky knoll above the river looks like an ideal camping spot, so we drag our tired bodies and gear up to it and build a fire to dry out. After the tension of our long day on the river, I feel like a coiled spring that has suddenly unwound. Each experience had added more strain without our realizing it, and by the time we arrived at Blue Ledge we were near exhaustion.

Our campsite is surrounded by pines and cedars; their fragrance mingles with smoke from our campfire. There are moss-covered ledges all around that would make an inviting place to flop down and snooze for days. But before that there is another urgency—food. Shortly the air is filled with the aroma of hot chicken soup and sizzling hamburgers with onions and beans. There are baked potatoes in the glowing coals, and a fresh salad with tomatoes and dressing, along with cheese and celery being passed around.

Dusk closes in, dwarfing our campfire's light within the yawning amphitheater. Blue Ledge's dark hulk looms like a mighty sentinel in the fading twilight, its sheer face echoing a muffled rumble from the Hudson. This is the throbbing heart of the Hudson—we have penetrated to its innermost sanctuary. A place of incomparable beauty appreciated more fully because of the effort it takes to get here—and the even greater effort needed to escape.

Our breakfast campfire is started in the early hours of dawn. Dampness has settled in the canyon, and mist flows along the river's surface like spooky fluid from another planet. Blue Ledge soars like a towering fortress, and the booming of rapids bounces down toward our tiny huddle of humanity as we scurry about, making preparations for the day. Someone shouts over the dull roar, "Look up!" The top of Blue Ledge glows a rosy pink, then golden. Then the first shafts of morning sunlight filter into the churning pit of mist. We push off from shore in our canoes and immediately turn down a corridor that seems to lead toward artillery fire.

The rapids below Blue Ledge defy description. The canyon walls narrow and the river funnels its volume in continuous, relentless drops over, around, and under gigantic boulders. It is impossible to shout in the din, and our only hope as a canoeing team lies in the reactions learned on our first day. The bow man must be alert to make immediate decisions and draw to either the right or left with lightning speed in order to avoid obstructions, while from the stern I try to pick a course down the choppy cataract.

Mile after mile without letup the violent pace continues. Each boat takes a turn at swamping, but luck is with us, and each time we are able to navigate the dumped canoe toward shore. It is an exhausting experience, however, and gradually the physical pressure mounts until one of our party makes a mistake and lands his canoe broadside against a large boulder. The upstream gunwale tips into the river and the canoe floods, folding around the rock. The two canoeists are thrown out but manage to swim to shore. We beach our crafts and all stand around, trying to figure out how we're going to get that canoe free.

Several attempts to get over to the swamped canoe fail. The force of the rushing water is unbelievable; there's just no way to wade or swim in such a current. Finally we unload one of the other canoes and carry it empty a few hundred yards upstream; then three of us get into the canoe. Two will paddle and approach the boulder, while the third man, who holds a coil of rope, will atempt to leap onto the rock as we backpaddle with all our might and slide by.

It works!

After some acrobatic maneuvers the third man is able to get the line around some solid superstructure on the canoe and toss the free end of the rope to shore. Now the five of us begin the task of hauling on the rope, but pull as we might, the canoe doesn't budge. A full canoe turned upstream is estimated to exert several tons of force.

So once again we take our empty canoe upstream and this time load a small log in the middle. Another member comes along to pass the log to the man on the rock as we go madly backpaddling by again. This works too.

Now with five of us on shore tugging on the rope and our man on the rock prying with the pole, the canoe begins to move ever so slowly from its trapped position. Inch by inch the canoe slides loose until, with one final heave, it is pulled free and swings like a big pendulum at the end of the rope to shore below us. The canoe is pretty well battered but still intact. It is a metal one, so with some pounding and bouncing up and down on it we manage to put it back into serviceable condition.

Meanwhile, our sixth man on the rock has been left marooned. Once again we tote the empty canoe upstream and float down over the rapids, backpaddling to slow our forward momentum. We shout for him to jump in as we go by. He nods that he understands, and we approach the boulder, flailing at the water as we go. He jumps. It doesn't work. He overshoots the canoe and falls into the water on the other side, nearly upsetting us in the process. But he's managed to hang on to the gunwale with one hand, so we float downstream, howling with laughter. The tension of struggling for several hours to free the boat has left us in a state of hysteria, and the comedy of our companion's misfortune was all that we needed to break the spell.

With that incident we crossed a threshold. Before, we had been too tense, paddling like machines, fighting the river instead of making it work for us. This didn't mean we had lost our respect for its power—far from it. Our experience with the swamped canoe on the rock reminded us not to drop our guard, but perhaps if our friends had been more relaxed as they worked around the rocks, the course of the water would have let them slip by without mishap.

The Hudson flows on, finally emerging into more open country as the hills recede and the valley widens. The Boreas River enters from the north just as the Hudson turns once again toward the south and, after a few miles, goes past the tiny village of North River. Here we pull our canoes up on shore for the last time—a tired, jubilant bunch, content with having passed through a place where few people ever venture. There is experience behind us, there is a land of living water, and we chuckle as we help our friends put their battered canoe on the car. Here is proof that we have been there.

Voices from the Sky

A mountain called Noonmark rises to a rather impressive pinnacle at the head of Keene Valley. Conical in appearance, it nestles within a cluster of rambling monarchs of the High Peak region. In spite of its stature, Noonmark doesn't rate the distinction of being called a High Peak—that is reserved for the elite group of forty-six mountains with altitude ranges above the 4000-foot contour. But Noonmark does have a sweeping view from its rocky summit that far surpasses most other peaks in the Adirondacks, so "eliteness" in this instance is of little consequence.

The Great Range, with its many-toothed summits, stretches across the northwestern skyline, terminating in the distant pyramids of Marcy and Haystack. Nearby, to the east, Giant Mountain soars like a mighty bulwark, its great western cirque raked by scars of colossal avalanches. Gathered around Noonmark's southern exposure is a collection of other high peaks dominated by the immense Dix Range.

I chose a quiet day late in April to hike up Noonmark. Parts of the trail were still choked with snow and ice, and even though a hint of spring had come to the valley below, the remnants from winter's deep freeze seemed reluctant to abandon their hold above. Tops of the Great Range and the other higher summits around me were obscured in dense cloud layer, but from my slightly lower elevation on Noonmark's summit I could look out under the clouds. It was a great sensation—I felt that if I had brought along a stepladder I could probably climb up it and stick my head in the cloud cover. As it was, standing on the very tip of Noonmark's pointed cone with sweeping valleys spread out below seemed profoundly elite—there was just no higher for me to go without banging my head on the ceiling.

Suddenly, from far away above the clouds, I detected a faint sound. At first I couldn't be sure; perhaps it was the wind playing tricks—it does sometimes, howling in the crags and crevices. I listened intently; then I heard it again, this time closer—voices from the sky! I strained my eyes toward the cloud cover, so close now I could almost reach up and touch it. The sound grew, and then, as if by magic, a string of dark objects appeared out of the vaporous ceiling. Dropping lower, the line of ghostly shapes lengthened and seemingly solidified. It was a formation of *Canada geese*! Their unmistakable honking call reached me clearly now, and a tingle went through me as all my senses came to attention. These birds were on their way home, back to nesting grounds in northern Canada. Their broad wings had carried them thousands of miles on a journey that held an incredible number of obstacles.

I stood dumfounded as the flock of about fifty majestic birds, cleaving the sky in classical V formation, came right for the top of Noonmark. I could see their distinctive white chin straps and hear the whooshing of great wings as they made a wide, sweeping turn a scant few feet above me. All the while they gabbled and talked among themselves, and then, stretching their long necks with determination, they swooped below the summit and disappeared toward Keene Valley. I listened in numb reverence long after they were out of earshot, hoping they might return, yet knowing the flock had vanished. All that remained was a haunting echo of their voices in my memory. In a brief particle of time the electrifying miracle of migration had passed through my life.

During the many years in which I've observed wildlife, the regal quality of Canada geese has always gripped my heart. They are born with an uncanny instinct for navigation, equipped with a sophisticated homing device that far surpasses man's electronic technology and mechanical gadgetry. To this day migration remains a baffling mystery. For my part, I'm content that it works—and that twice a year Canada geese fly through Adirondack country. In autumn the great birds tend to linger a bit on the abundance of lakes, marshes, and streams before the cold and the snows slowly push them southward. Their journey northward in spring is usually a little swifter as they are anxious to return to nesting areas and start their summer families. But during either trip the Adirondacks provide some of the richest waterways found anywhere along the eastern flyway, places within its remote regions where waterfowl of all species may enjoy an element of tranquillity.

The transient Canada geese grace Adirondack country with a comparatively short visitation. There is one seasonal resident, however, whose eerie call is even more memorable than that of the Canada goose. The great northern loon utters a mixture of yodeling gargles that sends chills up your spine. In all creation there are few sounds from the wild that touch your very soul as indelibly as its plaintive call.

People fortunate enough to hear a loon may never actually see one; the exception may be a fleeting glimpse on some remote pond or lake. The loon is strictly a water bird—its feet are set so far back on its body that the only way it can alight on land to nest is by sliding on its belly. But the loon makes up for this deficiency by being an accomplished swimmer, especially under water. Spotting a loon is a little like picking up mercury—just when you think you've got it, it disappears. To keep up with its underwater pattern is to engage in a baffling guessing game: the loon's next appearance is quite unpredictable. The loon's streamlined body and powerful pusher feet allow it to glide great distances beneath the water, ranking it supreme among diving birds.

There are hundreds of ponds and lakes throughout the region where loons range during summer and late fall before migrating southward. Many clusters of chain lakes with interconnecting waterways link vast areas into a living water haven where the loon selects its territorial residence. Time and again I have ventured back to these canoeing waters to hear the loon's melancholy reverberation pierce the stillness. Sometimes several loons scattered about enter into a calling contest in which they seem bent on outdoing each other. The shrill tattoo of their cries resounds through the forest and across the waters with such intensity that one would think there was a loon invasion.

I once took a tape recorder along on a canoe trip in the St. Regis region to see if I could pick up some of the loon's calls. We planned to go through a group of six remote ponds and lakes linked by short portages. One, called Bear Pond, has the clearest blue-green water I've seen anywhere in the Adirondacks. Gliding along over its surface in our canoes, we found it possible to see thirty or forty feet down into its incredibly pristine depths. One member of our party remarked that its clearness was actually frightening, for it would take only a slight push of man's thoughtlessness to upset the balance. As we neared shore I looked down and saw several beer cans shimmering along the bottom.

We put our campsite on a high knoll overlooking the pond. Enormous white pines and hemlocks wafted their fragrance in a late September breeze that whispered of the end of summer. Here and there, sprinkles of fire-red and gleaming gold thatched the evergreen wall. There was a nip in the air, but the spirit was invigorating. At night we sat around our campfire listening to the calls of loons echo all around. Even the great horned owls couldn't resist the sound and set up a chorus of their own. The mingling calls of the wild left us speechless.

Mist swirled off the pond as if from a vaporous vat when I launched my canoe in the morning. I placed my tape recorder in the bottom and paddled off in the direction of a cove from which I'd heard a loon call. The first shafts of sunlight streamed through towering pines along the shore and mottled the wispy pond surface with its radiance. My canoe drifted quietly, and I turned on my recorder to pick up the shrill wailing of a nearby loon lost from view in the fog. It was answered by another not far off my bow. The exchange continued for several minutes, and I could hardly contain myself at my good fortune in capturing this thrilling episode on tape. On an impulse I rewound the tape and tried a replay of the last few calls. As my recorder blasted out the very same notes the loons had uttered a few moments earlier, a sudden wild commotion burst upon the water all around my canoe. Two huge loons came flapping out of the mist, made repeated dives under my canoe, popped back up and stood right on end as they thrashed the water with their feet and burst forth with shrill gargling warnings. Hearing their own cries coming from the recorder, the loons must have thought strangers had invaded their territory, and they had therefore come out to defend their rights. Drenched in the splashing spray, I sat motionless while the frenzy continued. Then, as suddenly as they had come, the loons vanished. It was completely eerie. My canoe rocked gently as the ripples gradually diminished and the silent steam rose in golden spirals from the pond's surface. Pandemonium had evaporated as surely as the rising mist, and I was left with my thoughts—and a recording of an unrehearsed performance from the wild.

It's the unexpected surprises that add spice to Adirondack enjoyment. Once a friend and I took our canoe to explore the Eckford Chain near Blue Mountain. A series of lakes stretch out in a huge sweeping horseshoe that offers some of the finest canoeing waters anywhere. Blue Mountain Lake itself has a collection of tiny pine-covered islands at one corner and a nearby larger island where there is a camping spot. We set up for the night and were treated to a dazzling display of yellows, oranges, and reds as the setting sun melted behind the little pine-tufted islands. It was one of those quiet nights when wild sounds and color dissolve into a spiritual blending.

Blue Mountain Lake was not always that quiet. Few areas in the Adirondacks enjoy as colorful a history as that of the Blue Mountain–Raquette Lake sweep. Between 1880 and 1900 it was a booming summer resort region which eight or ten thousand people visited yearly. It was *the* place to go. Visitors arrived there by boat, train, or stage. Today its history is kept alive at the Adirondack Museum, which sits high on a bluff overlooking Blue Mountain Lake. The buildings of this fine museum house rare paintings, examples of early transportation, logging tools, ice harvesting equipment, delicate historical dioramas, and an incomparable collection of guide boats and canoes. The Memorial Boat Building itself is uniquely Adirondack—nothing like it exists anywhere else in the world today.

In the morning we were awakened by a loud splash in the lake just off the tip of our island camp. I jumped out of my sleeping bag and rushed over to the water's edge. Our camping spot was covered by a thick canopy of evergreen trees that screened out most of the view, so it was necessary to be at the shoreline in order to see anything. A big cedar leaned out over the water—I stood on its curved trunk to get a better look at the lake now emerging in the light of a new day. All was quiet and calm except for a telltale circle of ripples about a hundred yards out. I looked in all directions but couldn't figure out what had made the sound.

All of a sudden a flashing object in the sky caught my eye. At the same moment whatever it was dropped like a comet toward the lake, hitting with a loud impact and sending up a shower of water. An instant later it emerged, but this time its speed was reduced to a struggling slow motion of big flapping wings as it fought to gain altitude. It was an osprey. At first I was so excited I thought it was a bald eagle because of its big white head, but after I'd caught my breath and looked closer I could see its definite characteristics—an all-white belly and a kink in its wings as it flew.

The osprey is sometimes called a fish hawk, and this morning I was being treated to a classic demonstration of its habits. After it had reached some altitude, the osprey began to hover in one spot by beating its wings. It let out a series of sharp staccato whistles; then, plummeting like a streak, it plunged feet first into the lake. Even the best of wild creatures has its bad moments. Once again it emerged without its quarry. The osprey made repeated dives without luck. Each time it came back up out of the lake, it deliberately shook itself in flight, sending a shower of water in all directions. As I watched from the concealment of the cedars, I was spellbound by its performance.

Each time the osprey dove, it moved a little closer in my direction. I was so absorbed in its antics that this subtle tactic had escaped my detection until I suddenly realized there was a shallow gravel bar offshore. It may or may not have been planned, but I think that fish hawk was driving its quarry to shallow waters on purpose, because in one final dive it landed where the water was only a foot or so deep, and with a great thrashing fury emerged with a good-sized trout. Then, with sharp cheeping whistles, it spread its great wings and flew off to the distant tall pines on the farther islands to enjoy its breakfast.

Such privileged moments are few. The chance opportunity to be at the right place at the right time to view such a wildlife drama may come only once in a lifetime. The light had not developed enough for me to take any photographs, so all I could do was sit there with my camera in my hands and absorb the wondrous incident in my memory. Images can be captured on film, but the thrilling moment when you hear those voices in the sky is something no photographer can duplicate.

Mountaintop Treasures

A distant rumble warned me of an approaching storm, so I hastened my pace up the last quarter of a mile of Skylight. Barren mountaintops are no place to be in an electrical storm, but I was hoping to photograph some rare alpine plants that grow above timberline, so I raced for the summit before the remaining rays of sunshine disappeared.

Skylight is one of the remotest peaks in the Adirondacks. Isolated south of Mount Marcy, it ranks fourth in height at slightly under 5000 feet elevation. Its rocky top is like a plateau and encompasses several acres above timberline. Scattered clumps of stunted evergreens mingle with grassy patches and miniature bogs among loose boulders and open ledges. In the botanical world, grassy patches and bogs are referred to as "communities" and contain plants which adapt to certain kinds of environmental existence. On Skylight, the sedge meadows, heath rush, snowbanks, and wind-exposed areas are communities that support plant growth. The Alpine plants here are unique in this region, thriving only on summits where the harsh conditions are similar to those of their habitual terrain in the Arctic. Flowers are tiny and delicate, and most have a very short blooming period. The best time to see their colorful display is usually between mid-May and late June.

When I reached the timberline, shafts of sunlight were winking in and out of ragged forerunner clouds driven by a towering thunderhead glowering to the west. Bulging black appendages from it had already devoured nearby mountains, and I knew it was only a matter of time before the cloak of clouds would descend upon me. In the little hummocks of grass thrashed by gusts of wind, I caught a fleeting glimpse of bright color at some distance.

As I dashed across the ledges, I saw the dazzling magenta of Lapland rosebay quaking in the wind. Its brilliant blossoms resemble miniature rhododendron flowers. The leaves are narrow and leathery, and the whole plant is speckled with rusty spots. Lapland rosebay is one of the more conspicuous alpine flowers found above timberline.

As I knelt down to photograph it, I was startled to find that I had almost squashed some tiny diapensia blossoms. Like most alpine flowers, these plants are so small you have to get on your hands and knees to examine them. Often hikers so absorbed in the view will unknowingly walk right over the blossoms.

Diapensia forms rounded mats or cushions of thickly clustered minute leaves. The flowers, about the size of a dime, are white, have five petals, and stand on clove-like stalks above the cushion of leaves.

The rumbling of thunder was growing louder, so I looked around in a hurry. I wanted to find and photograph as many flowers as I could before the storm broke. Shrubs of Labrador tea were scattered all over, their clusters of white blossoms bobbing like ping-pong balls in the breeze. The shrub has elongated evergreen leaves that curl up and have a dense brown woolly coating underneath. The flowers are very tiny and grow in a small ball or clump at the ends of the branches. Labrador tea is one of the taller heaths. I took a couple of quick shots just as the sunlight disappeared.

I could see tufts of cotton grass—sometimes called hare's tail—scattered about in the bogs. It's a grasslike sedge that is easily recognizable because of its cottony seed heads bobbing in the wind.

The bogs themselves are often quite small. A mountaintop bog may be no bigger than a teacup, or it may be hundreds of feet across. The important thing is that the bogs support life, most often on a miniature scale. For example, the wrens egg cranberry grows as a baby vine with flowers not much bigger than a pinhead and shaped like a shooting star. It really takes close examination to find these minute plants camouflaged among tussocks of grass.

Suddenly thunder and lightning crashed together with shattering impact. The storm was upon me and I had to get out of the open quickly.

As I scampered across the ledges, with big fat drops splashing down, my eye caught a little patch of pink in a shallow depression. Better judgment urged me to move on, but my curiosity dominated, so I ran over to take a closer look. Bending down on all fours, I realized I had discovered the most delicate treasure of all, the fragile flowers of alpine azalea. Certainly the rarest of all Adirondack alpine plants, this dwarf shrub has evergreen leaves with stems that creep along the ground forming a mat no more than a quarter of an inch high. Its pink blossoms, which are about the size of a matchhead, stand upright on transparent red stalks. It was frustrating to find this nest of beauties at the last possible moment. I wanted to linger and study them more closely, but there was time for only two quick photos before a drenching downpour swooped across Skylight's summit. I raced below timberline as a blinding flash of lightning streaked through the air followed by a clap of thunder that made my ears ring.

In another half mile I reached a lean-to between the Marcy–Skylight col where I found shelter from the sheets of pouring rain. In spite of my soaking, there was the inner satisfaction of having found and photographed some of the Adirondack mountaintop treasures.

Falling Waters

There are thousands of lacy cascades and waterfalls scattered throughout Adirondack country. Many are hidden deep within ravines and inaccessible gorges, while others spout from cliff faces or tumble down long staircases of mossy ledges. Because the mountains and lowlands are enshrouded in a vast timberland, the Adirondacks hold water like a mammoth sponge. The entire region is a giant watershed in which the life-giving liquid may be found even in the driest of seasons.

In springtime the number of falls is dramatically increased by melting snow. Lichen-covered ledges which are dry in summer often become raceways for innumerable cascades during the early runoff. Freshets bubble from mountainsides feeding rocky streambeds; their brimful banks channel the dancing water like natural sluiceways. Major brooks and rivers flood to enormous proportions, and any ordinary waterfall along the way becomes a spectacular display of thundering power.

Having explored Adirondack country for many years, I have seen a number of its great and small waterfalls. Lots of them can be viewed along the roadsides and from trails or canoe routes, but that barely scratches the surface compared to the number tucked away in remote places. To see some of the beauties one must expend considerable energy and penetrate some wild areas.

Such is the case for one of the most intriguing and perhaps unique falls of its kind found anywhere in the world. It is located in Avalanche Pass, a deep notch between towering cliffs on Mount Colden and the MacIntyre Range. A trail does provide ingress, and where it winds up through the gap and reaches the height of land within the pass, a waterfall tumbles from a niche high on its wall. A rock jutting from the wall cleaves

41

the falling water into two streamers, and the runoff in turn flows in two different directions.

Unusual in itself but of particular significance is that the rock's precise location happens by a curious quirk of nature to fall on the exact boundary between two separate watersheds—the St. Lawrence and the Hudson. From its division, one stream flows down Avalanche Pass on its northeastern side to Marcy Brook, through the Ausable River, and out to Lake Champlain. The Richelieu River is born at Champlain's outlet, and it in turn empties into the St. Lawrence. On the other side, the second stream drops down the southwestern end of Avalanche Pass and through several small lakes to the Opalescent River, where it joins the Hudson and eventually flows out to sea at New York City. I daresay there are few places on earth where nature has arranged a waterfall's division with such precision.

Not far from Avalanche Pass, on the Hudson's drainage side, is Avalanche Lake, jammed between precipitous cliffs that rise directly out of the water. Countless avalanches roaring down the mountain's flank have left massive open scars. Any severe rainstorm may send a deluge of sheet waterfalls rushing down the avalanche paths, scouring the mountainside in their awesome plunge.

In a steep walled gorge slicing a trough up the side of Mount Colden, a trap dike was formed in aeons past by molten rock which was injected into a fissure of harder strata and then weathered away to become what is now a yawning chimney. In wet times the dike acts as a drain spout, as it discharges a vertical river from Colden's face.

A few ranges southeast, in a valley by Lower Ausable Lake, Rainbow Falls plummets down a 150-foot cliff into a narrow chasm. In spring, vapor generated by its gigantic thundering pours from the grotto like a small rainstorm. On a few occasions when I tried to hike up the narrow ravine that cradles the cataract, I became drenched long before actually seeing the falls. Later in summer, when its volume diminishes, Rainbow Falls seemingly flows in slow motion, releasing lacy veils that seem to vaporize and disappear. There is only one way to describe Rainbow Falls—it is a majestic natural spectacle.

42

It is, however, rivaled by one other—O.K. Slip Falls in the heart of Hudson Gorge country. O.K. Slip bursts from a forest-mantled fissure plunging free for 200 feet before striking a jumble of rocks at its base in a whopping shower of spray. O.K. Slip Falls, hidden in a rugged area resembling a jungle, has been seen only by a privileged few hardy enough to venture to its remote domain.

Not all Adirondack falls are as difficult to reach. Roads provide easy access to many fine examples, such as crystal-clear Split Rock on the Bouquet River near Elizabethtown. A few miles north, Roaring Brook drops from the base of Giant Mountain in a 100-foot display that may be viewed from the highway to Keene Valley. In the western reaches of Adirondack country, St. Regis Falls makes an impressive drop as it passes below the village of its namesake. Farther south, between Forked Lake and Long Lake, the Raquette River spills over a barrier of ledges in delicate streamers to form Buttermilk Falls. And at Luzerne the mighty Hudson makes a sharp turn, crashing over cliffs just before swirling under a bridge.

It would be hard to imagine such a vast watershed without its lively cataracts. Adirondack country is blessed with a fair share of falling waters.

Trekking by Shoe and Ski

Frozen ponds and lakes are like collection cups for frigid air when the winter wind subsides in Adirondack high country. Sometimes the temperature plummets on calm nights and makes you wonder where all that mercury in the thermometer's little glass tube goes. In the clear, crisp air more stars appear to fill the sky than ever before, squeezing together in a dome of sparkling splendor. Balsams and spruces soar upward like black daggers toward the icy points of light, and from somewhere in the forest's inky thicket a great horned owl's chilling hoot shatters the silence.

On such a night on Moose Pond, deep in the High Peak region, seven of us were tenting on our first lap of the Northville-Placid trail—on a ski trip. Earlier in the day we had started from Averyville, a tiny parking spot at the end of a plowed road just a few miles south of Lake Placid village. With a clear sky and firmly packed snow, we clipped off the miles, arriving at tiny Moose Pond just before darkness. The only lean-to was occupied by a couple of trappers who had winterized the shelter with a plastic front covering, a door, a wood stove, and some other conveniences, such as tables and chairs. They kindly offered us space in their snug quarters, but we chose to pitch our tents on the pond's snowy surface. It was our first night out, and we were frisky, intent on conditioning ourselves for our long trek.

Before settling in for the night, the trappers treated us to tales of wolves roaming the woods. "There's wolves out there, all right. Seen a pack of 'em the other day jest roamin' 'round.'' I was rather skeptical, but this spicy bit of news instilled apprehension in some of the younger members of our group. Coming in, we had seen a lot of "big dog" tracks along frozen beaver ponds. In some places there appeared to be quite a gathering of tracks, but mostly they seemed to wander aimlessly back and forth. I was sure of one thing: wolves like those found in the Yukon had long since disappeared from the Adirondacks. Chances are the trappers had seen coyotes. A new breed has recently been filtering into the Northeast—a sort of mixture of wild dog and Western coyote. At any rate, sharing a cross-country skiing trip with "wolves" was an interesting and somewhat different prospect.

In the middle of the night I was awakened by a loud *crack*—a sharp report like that of a rifle. I sat bolt upright in my sleeping bag. I was sure the wolves were upon us and that the trappers were defending us. All was silent; then I heard another *crack*, this time farther away. Now fully awake, I recognized it as the popping of pitch in evergreen trees. In extremely low temperatures pitch pockets in spruces, balsams, and pines freeze and expand, sometimes causing the wood fibers to shatter from the strain. The result is often a loud noise like that of a rifle shot.

I poked my head out of the tent to check the thermometer. Twenty below! No wonder the pitch was popping! Perhaps we should have taken advantage of the trappers' hospitality.

Still, I had confidence in our group's equipment. The chances of finding a winterized shelter in the Adirondacks is remote indeed, so we had packed for every eventuality—or so it seemed. Our sleeping bags were good to thirty below, tents were lightweight and strong, and our cross-country equipment in top shape. With these aces up our sleeve, we felt we could cope with anything the Adirondacks had to offer.

The Northville–Placid trail is well suited to that kind of challenge. It is the longest continuous trail in the region, penetrating some hundred and thirty miles of rugged country. We chose to ski it from north to south after a careful study of contour maps revealed that the least amount of altitude gain occurred in that direction. The trail generally follows an easy gradient except for the section around Blue Mountain, where it climbs some steep pitches. In its entire length the trail is traversed only a few times by highways. We planned to use these crossings to solve the logistics of carrying food. In winter, body needs are much more than those of a casual summer hike, so paring down a pack's load in cold weather is a problem. Bulky clothing, parkas, hats, mittens, fuel, and gas stoves take up space ordinarily used for food during less strenuous trips. As a result, an extended winter trek can become quite an ordeal just through the necessity of transporting a lot of equipment. So, by using two cars, we divided the trip into segments and kept food in one of the vehicles. At the end of each segment, two drivers would return in one car to the point of departure, pick up the second car, then shuttle both cars on to positions in the next section.

The morning of the second day was bitterly cold, and breaking camp was a numbing experience. Tents were stiff, sleeping bags wouldn't stuff into their sacks, and our fingers and toes were like blocks of wood. Comfort came in the form of a tiny gas stove that purred softly and on which we prepared oatmeal and hot fruit. Our trapper friends were still fast asleep in their warm lean-to by the time we hefted our packs and started off on the next lap toward Duck Hole. Chances are the wolves were sacked out somewhere too, for we never got a glimpse of them.

From Moose Pond the trail takes a gentle downgrade following a twisting stream through balsam and alder thickets for several miles before emerging at Duck Hole. There the Adirondacks' allure suddenly unfolds. Nestled among corrugated wooded ridges and ringed by dark spires of spruce and balsam, Duck Hole in its hushed silence gives you a deep sense of solitude, accompanied by a feeling of accomplishment at having penetrated to the heart of a wilderness land.

A gusting wind picked up as we skied between tiny tufts of islands growing out of the pond's snowy surface. I noticed that it was a warm wind, quite a marked change from the below-zero readings we had experienced a few hours earlier. By the time we finished lunch at a lean-to along the shore, it had moderated even more. The sky took on an ominous dull gray color, and I wondered if we were in for a weather change.

We began the long Cold River Valley section. From Duck Hole the trail takes a nice downhill run for a mile or so, then climbs from the riverbed to follow a higher elevation. Zigzagging around a series of connecting beaver ponds, we made a mistake in attempting shortcuts across the ponds and became hopelessly entangled in thickets of dead trees and twisted alders. On our maps it looked like a good idea, but in practice, burdened with skis and bulky packs, we found it a time-consuming and exhausting experience. To add to the complications, the snow was becoming sticky and we constantly had to clean chunks off the bottom of our skis.

Eventually we picked up the route again and descended to Cold River, which lay muffled under an enormous blanket of snow. Large wet flakes began to fall, and we struggled along, alternating between stretches of skiing on the river and on the trail that parallels it. Darkness was closing in as the snow turned to rain—then through the mist we saw the outline of a lean-to. The shelter was a welcome sight, and it was a relief to know we wouldn't have to pitch tents in the winter downpour. Rain is a serious crippler on any winter excursion, and we were many miles from the comfort of drying facilities, so the lean-to offered a pretty good opportunity to set up housekeeping.

Making a campfire is no easy task when every available stick is either frozen or soaked, but somehow we managed to get one going and partially dried out our clothes. We still relied on our gas stove to cook our supper on —it's the only dependable means of heating food on a trek. After we'd been soaked to the bone, nothing ever tasted so good as that big pot of beef stew and the hot chocolate we had. Slightly warmer and drier, we crawled into our sleeping bags and fell asleep to the unseasonal sound of rain.

The morning of our third day was damp and miserable. The rain had stopped temporarily, but trees and bushes were soggy and dripping. In twenty-four hours the temperature had risen a staggering fifty-eight degrees from twenty below zero to thirty-eight above! We rose from our clammy sleeping bags, stuffed our wet gear into our packs while preparing breakfast, then began the grueling exodus to Long Lake through saturated snow.

Cold River seemed endless. Under most conditions it would have been a delightful run over the snow-choked stream winding between a wall of evergreens, but within a few miles a misty rain began to fall and once again we were sloshing along in soaking boots and parkas. There was another urgency in our getting out that day—our next food supplies were some twenty miles away in our car at Long Lake village and we had used up almost all the food planned for the first segment of our trip.

The gentle river gradient was of little advantage with the sticky snow conditions. We just couldn't seem to make any time. None of the ski waxes worked well, and we had to stop every few yards to scrape off big clumps of snow. Finally we stopped and fired our gas stove, heated the bottoms of the skis, then scraped all the old wax off and applied new klisters. These tube waxes are supposed to work for most difficult conditions, but we still couldn't find the right combination and continued to bog down.

It was midafternoon when we reached the northern tip of Long Lake, an exhausted bunch with ten miles still to go down the lake to the village. The misty rain had stopped, however, and now the temperature began to drop. The skiing had improved, but the wind picked up and started to blow toward us. We transferred packs from the women to the stronger men and pushed onward into the bitter wind.

The ten-mile stretch down Long Lake's exposed expanse was later referred to as our "death march." Large puddles of water that had formed on the lake's snowy surface were now refreezing. Slushy snow began to pile up like concrete, this time accumulating on the tops of our skis and jamming the bindings—we made periodic attempts to pry it loose with our poles. Everyone's boots were like frozen lumps of wood, and the packs were stiff as boards.

We moved mechanically now, peering through the gathering darkness for some glimpse of the end, but it eluded us like a mirage. The white lake melted to a dirty gray and blowing snow began to fall, obscuring the way even more. Every muscle screamed with each stride. We fought an overwhelming desire to lie down in the snow and quit. Heads lowered, we slogged on, sparked by the single thought that we were not alone in our agony and that strength lay in our combined chain of humanity trailing over the lake.

And then, through the swirling snow, we saw a faint light on the shore. It grew brighter as we advanced, and finally we could make out the outline of a house. We staggered to the door and were warmly welcomed inside. We looked like a mighty bedraggled bunch, but our heartfelt appreciation was surely evident as we sprawled out on our host's floor. It was nearly nine o'clock—thirteen long hours since the beginning of our day's journey in the fickle elements. The outcome had been fortunate. We had slipped from the clutches of a really bad situation—an experience that taught us never to underestimate changeable Adirondack weather.

Our car and food supplies were only a short distance up the road, so while our newfound benefactors prepared hot soup and other goodies, I went to retrieve it.

Through the night and all the next day rain and snow alternated and eventually became a full-fledged ice storm. We abandoned the rest of our plans. As we drove home, we saw many streams that had been peaceful and snow-covered were turned into open sluices for icy torrents. Our thoughts wandered back to Cold River, and we wondered what it was like now, just twenty-four hours later.

Winter travel in the Adirondacks is serious business. Weather conditions vary from day to day, or may, as illustrated by our Northville–Lake Placid trek, change from hour to hour. Snowstorms sometimes dump enormous amounts of fresh snow, making progress difficult for those breaking trail. A sudden thaw and freezing rain may turn the back country into a squishy mess, with flooded rivers that cannot be crossed. Another dangerous factor is the terrain—deep valleys, steep slopes, blowdowns, spruce thickets, icy summit cones, precipitous drop-offs—you name it and chances are the Adirondacks have it.

Invariably newcomers ask, "Should I travel on snowshoes or use cross-country skis?" The answer lies with the individual and a study of the intended terrain, but there are other factors to be considered that can be evaluated only by experience. The Adirondacks are a special world, and the problems they present to winter travelers are as varied as the mountains themselves.

During my ten years of association with the Adirondack Winter Mountaineering School at Heart Lake, I worked with some of the finest mountaineers in eastern America. Snowshoes, skis, and crampons were our keys to wilderness penetration, but no matter how adept we became, there was always something to learn from each new adventure.

49

There are many trails suitable for cross-country skiing, but snow-shoes are recommended for places off the beaten track. Whenever we plan to go above timberline, we carry a pair of crampons in our pack for use on the exposed areas, which are usually icy. Some climbers prefer to have an ice ax, too, as an aid on the steep pitches and to steady them in a strong wind.

My first ascent of an Adirondack peak on skis many years ago was a lesson I shall never forget. I had driven into Keene one night during a quiet snowstorm. Usually there is a lot of blowing wind and drifting snow in the mountains, but this was an exceptional night, with soft flakes fluttering like millions of tiny butterflies. During "quiet snows" it's possible to hear the crystals landing. They have a way of building up to quite an accumulation, so that by morning the entire landscape is smothered under a thick blanket.

My companions and I started off to climb a mountain called Big Slide—they were on snowshoes, I was on skis. Big Slide is one of the 4000-footers that guard Johns Brook Valley, just opposite the Great Range. I had a brand-new pair of cross-countries, plus climbing skins, which I was anxious to demonstrate for the benefit of my seasoned Adirondack snowshoers.

Skins are climbing aids used principally by ski-mountaineers. Made of sealskin or synthetic fiber, they are attached to the running surface of the skis with straps and buckles and are easily removed when the skier is ready to descend. The skin's fibers lie in such a way that the ski slides easily over the snow as you move forward, but grabs the surface to prevent sliding backward as you climb.

Within the first mile I felt that my hunch about the choice of equipment was right. My companions began to wallow in deep snow up the first pitch—a series of knobs called The Brothers. Meanwhile, I was having a merry old time going straight up the slope on my skis and climbing skins. I was convinced this was the combination for zipping up and down all the Adirondack peaks. Snowshoers use a technique called "kicking steps" when they ascend steep grades. In moderately firm snow, step-kicking isn't too difficult, but in deep new snow it can be an exhausting chore, especially if you're leading and breaking trail. This was the problem my companions faced on the ridge leading to Big Slide.

After several hours of climbing I reached the top and sat smugly waiting for them to arrive and remark how great it must be on skis—but they never said a word when at last they reached the summit too. Either they were envious or knew something that I didn't. I was soon to learn the hard way that zipping up is one thing, but coming down is something else! At first on the way down I didn't do too badly, but Adirondack trails are narrow—so narrow, in fact, that you can't do a snowplow, much less turn to stop. The underbrush and evergreens are so thick along the sides that it is impossible to zigzag off the trail in most places. My ungainly descent became a wild, whirling windmill of skis, poles, and pack as I came crashing after the snowshoers, who were now enjoying a controlled glissade down the packed trail. In desperation I donned my climbing skins and tried backing down the more difficult places, frantically clutching at trees as I descended in this unorthodox position. The result was always the same: I ended in a heap, buried under a tangle of branches and skis. In places the trail widened enough for me to sidestep, and there were even some modest pitches that I could swoop down, but the sudden drop-offs or hidden corners sent me sprawling. In the end I came straggling off the mountain looking like a snowball that had bounded from top to bottom.

In succeeding years I learned to calculate my ski-mountaineering trips more carefully, even to the point of carrying a pair of snowshoes in my pack for more difficult terrain higher up. And during many snowshoe trips I learned that snowshoes provide more control than skis and are indispensable on trailless peaks where the trees grow very close together. Certainly they are better for breakable crust—snow that has a thin film of either ice or frozen snow on its surface.

There are many places where cross-countries are quite an advantage for clipping off the miles, especially on old logging roads or over frozen chain lakes. There are some mountains within the Adirondacks where they may be used successfully, but an experience such as mine on Big Slide has a way of making me look before I leap—the terrain is a deciding factor, but for the most part snowshoes have it for winter ascents.

51

The Thin Cold Edge

Is it safe to be way up there in the mountains?" That's a question frequently debated by those who never climb or who don't understand mountains. The Adirondack High Peaks look especially formidable in winter—and they *are* formidable for the inexperienced. But my contention has always been that the most dangerous part of mountaineering is the drive on the highways to get there.

Still, the elements in winter deserve a healthy respect. In a matter of minutes tranquil conditions may deteriorate to a serious situation. Areas above timberline are particularly subject to sudden changes. A party which at one moment may be enjoying the view may in the next be groping along in a blinding white-out. Routes above timberline lose all definition, and traces of tracks vanish with blowing and drifting snow. The party may wander helplessly and stray in a wrong direction into an impenetrable wilderness of blowdowns and thickets. Add plummeting temperatures and exhaustion, and the frigid jaws of winter slowly tighten.

Trails are vital lifelines for winter travelers, but at best many of them are poorly marked. In winter the actual grade is usually buried under several feet of snow, and the terrain looks the same in all directions. Evergreen trees at higher elevations are often encased in snow, and the heavily laden branches dip down to form a labyrinth of chambers and tunnels. Even a rabbit has a hard time finding its way around. Precipitous cliffs, deep chasms, and a tangle of twisted trees are just a few more complications that may be encountered if a party goes astray.

But the High Peaks beckon, and each year more and more people venture to this winter wilderness. Experience is best acquired by listening and by doing, so back in the late 1950s the Adirondack Mountain Club established a Winter Mountaineering School at Heart Lake, a few miles south of Lake Placid village. Each season during Christmas vacation students gather from all over the Northeast to take part in a program designed to inculcate greater understanding of the mountains and develop winter mountaineering skills. Beginners and advanced climbers alike have an opportunity to participate in training programs conducted by experienced instructors, which include training in the use of snowshoes, touring skis, ice ax, and crampons. Special emphasis is placed on high-energy foods and on clothing and other equipment. Workshops are held with instruction in ice climbing, emergency shelters, and many other cold-weather subjects. The program is geared toward safer winter mountaineering.

For a number of years I was an instructor at the school. Taking part in many of its activities gave me a chance to explore many of the Adirondacks' least accessible areas. The mountains were our training grounds, and we ranged to some of their most remote regions. Overnight trips were often taken above timberline where students experienced conditions similar to those sometimes found on major expeditions.

One of our early adventures took place on Algonquin Peak. At slightly under a mile in altitude, it is the second highest peak and is conveniently situated near the school's base of operations at Heart Lake. I was leading a party of seven seasoned mountaineers over its exposed summit cone when we were suddenly engulfed by a violent storm. Since we were on a planned overnight trip, we had all the necessary equipment to bivouac, so we pitched our tents at the edge of timberline just as darkness set in. From our tiny perch clinging to the mountainside we could hear the wind howl like an express train over Algonquin's frozen summit. Flying chunks of ice bombarded our campsite with the force of fractured shrapnel. The gale mounted in ferocity, and I wondered if our battered tents could withstand the continuous barrage that threatened to rip us from the slope.

Retreat was out of the question. Once darkness was upon us, the best decision was to sit tight, content to have warm sleeping bags—which in winter are the only link to life in an overnight survival. It was frightfully cold. I struggled with the zipper on the tent's front flap—it was jammed. Our tent was an old one with a metal zipper (some of the newer ones have nylon zippers), and condensation from our bodies inside had frozen in its teeth. After a while I was able to work it loose. Then, with my mittened hand, I reached out to feel for the snowshoes I had jammed in the snow next to our tent. I had tied a small thermometer to one of the straps. Shining my flashlight through the opening, I squinted at the bit of red mercury which had sunk nearly out of sight. It read thirty-five degrees below zero!

The next tent was pitched only a few feet away, so I yelled over to find out how they were doing. The screeching gale sucked up my voice and scattered it in the wind. Finally after repeated tries I heard a faint response. "What's your temperature?" I bellowed. Again I poked my flashlight out and shone it in the direction of the other tent. Someone's head appeared in the opening, and I could barely make out his words through the racket of wind and flying ice. "Thirty-five below!" That did it—two thermometers registering the same. It was mighty cold. Combined with wind chill produced by hurricane-force winds battering the mountain, it could well have added up to one hundred degrees below zero. We were on the thin cold edge of survival.

We tried to communicate some more by yelling at the top of our lungs, but our friends might just as well have been on the moon. The screaming storm made it impossible to hear across the scant five feet that separated our tents.

So now we made preparations in our tent for some hot soup. First, snow had to be melted on our gas stoves to provide water. However, the air was so cold that steam rising from the pot immediately condensed in fine particles that swirled around inside the tent like a miniature snowstorm. Within minutes it was impossible to see two inches in front of us, and we groped around like blind men. The inevitable happened—we accidentally kicked over the pot of partially melted snow and the water spilled out on the tent floor. On hands and knees, we felt around for the water, trying to scoop it up before it soaked our clothing. A curious thing happened—the water solidified in an instant, and even though some had landed on our sleeping bags, it never wet them in its frozen state. We started the melting process once again. A swirling cloud of crystals resulted; as before, we were unable to see anything.

54

Suddenly I realized the pot had upset again, this time knocked over by the belching tent heaving in and out from furious blasts of the storm. It seemed useless to continue, so we gathered up our latest batch of ice and flung it outside, then ate our supper cold.

All night long the violent wind continued its relentless drive. I'm sure none of us slept too well, thinking that each gust might tear the tents from the mountainside. In the morning the wind abated somewhat, and we made preparations to break camp. The temperature had risen slightly to thirty below. In extreme cold the process of packing up is a frustrating experience in which every operation is a laborious effort. Sleeping bags don't seem to fit back in their stuff bags, and stuffing them with clumsy mittens on your hands is an awkward business. Boots are solid blocks, and once you put them on, you feel as if your feet were in little refrigerators. The worst part is taking down tents that are frozen stiff and bend like sheet metal. The problem of fastening snowshoe straps and buckles can be maddening. If you remove your mittens for even a moment to fuss with them, your fingers become instantly numb.

After two hours we were under way, released from the mountain's grasp and a wild night's experience that taught us respect for the High Peaks in winter. On our return to the school's base of operations, we found that winds of more than ninety miles an hour had been recorded in nearby Lake Placid. It is conceivable that the wind velocity might have exceeded a hundred miles an hour on Algonquin.

Other trips at lower elevations didn't fare so well—there were many cases of frostbite, but in the end all recovered without serious complications. In such severe conditions wind chill is rapid and absolute; proper clothing is the only salvation. In the years that followed, we found that much was gained by our early experiences and pioneering in winter mountaineering. Guidelines were developed and recommended for safer trips in penetrating deeply into remote regions of the Adirondacks. A minimum party, for example, is considered to be no less than four; that way, if someone is injured, two can return for help while the fourth remains with the victim. A heavy-weight sleeping bag is regarded as essential on all day trips of any extended duration. There is no such thing as stopping somewhere in the woods and building a fire to keep warm. Every stick of wood is permeated with frozen water and frost, making it impossible to start a fire without a blowtorch.

Clothing plays a vital role in winter excursions. Loose-fitting garments, preferably wool, are the best. Down parkas, hoods, windbreakers, face masks, extra mittens and socks are just a few of the essentials for those who venture deep into Adirondack country.

The need to carry extra clothing, even on a day trip, was brought home with stunning impact on another of my earlier expeditions. Ice climbing was in its infancy, and in our search for new routes we used the great western cirque of Giant Mountain as one of our favorite training areas. Giant presents one of the most formidable faces in the Adirondacks. Both its east and west flanks have been raked by scouring avalanche paths, leaving long open scars that make ideal avenues for ice climbers to scale the mountain.

Ice climbing is a team effort, done by two or as many as four on a rope. The indispensable items of equipment are crampons and ice ax. Crampons, or "climbing irons," are metal spikes about an inch and a quarter long and are secured to climbing boots with straps or nylon thongs. They must fit snugly—a loose crampon on an icy slope can spell trouble. The ice ax has a hardwood shaft with a metal spike at the handle end and a head that is combination adz and pick. The adz blade is about two inches wide, and sharp. The pick is about seven inches long, and also sharp. It is an absolutely essential aid in climbing and descending on ice. No single piece of equipment carries so much responsibility. When climbers have not "roped up," the ice ax provides the individual with the gear he needs to make a self-arrest. Varying ice and slope conditions might require variations of the basic technique for making self-arrests, but without an ice ax it is nearly impossible to stop a fall.

Depending on the angle, climbing as a roped party is the safest way to make ascents. If the climbers travel in unison and one falls, the others must be alert to drive their axes into the snow, or whatever is immediately handy, to anchor themselves and bring their fellow climber to a stop on the rope. When the slope or angle is severe or the quality of footing questionable, a roped party sets up a "belay," in which one climber moves while the others are "tied-in" to a secure projection, to boulders, trees, or some other kind of ice anchor. Each nonmoving member of the party takes a firm stance, which may be with the aid of his ice ax, and then passes the rope around his body to create arresting friction as he lets the rope out or takes it in to accommodate the moving climber until he reaches a safe stance. Thus a party ascends a slope under complete control.

A number of the slides on Giant have names, and I was leading a party on one called The Eagle. I was near the top, working on an intricate bulge of ice where the exposure was rather frightening. My comrades had taken up belay stances off to one side while I hacked away some steps with my ice ax. Suddenly, when I drove my pick into the blue-green ice, water that must have been under terrific pressure squirted out like a fire hose, soaking me in my precarious position, hitting me with such force that it knocked me from the wall. In a wild clatter of scraping crampons and flailing ice ax I flipped backward down the slope but fortunately was tethered to the rope. It swung me in an arc like a pendulum below my climbing partners. Without that lifeline I could have been a goner, but the incident happened without injury and all I ended up with was a good soaking. That in itself could have been serious, since we were working in below-zero weather, but the lesson of taking extra clothing along paid off and I made a quick change.

Perhaps the most significant lesson in ice climbing—or in any other remote penetration into the Adirondacks, for that matter—is the need for responsible comrades. Mountaineers are a special breed. Most of them have positive ideas and as a consequence will sometimes clash in their convictions. You may have parallel interests and agree on principles but still be completely apart on methods. Ice climbing is likely to involve situations in which responsible comrades are extremely important. Unlike a casual snowshoe trip, climbing is an advanced category of travel requiring technical know-how that is more than just an arbitrary set of rules. High-angle climbing in sub-zero weather calls for unshaken confidence in your companions, for you are mutually dependent. Once you've crossed that invisible thin, cold edge, you need them as much as they need you.

Farewell to Fall

Every Adirondack season has qualities that make it special, but autumn is unquestionably the most vibrant. During its early stages vivid hues of red and yellow tinge summer greens with random splashes of color. Like a blotter, the foliage rapidly absorbs the splashes, and the entire countryside is soon saturated with blazing brilliance. At higher elevations ridges and ravines fold into mauve and gold pierced by the dark spikes of evergreens and flood downward in patterns that rival the most intricate Persian rug. Brooks that gushed with the force of spring runoff are now mere trickles coursing their quiet ways, reflecting the bursting canopy of leaves in their shallow pools. The air is crisp and invigorating, and the summer's pesky gnats and mosquitoes have disappeared.

In time, temperatures begin a downward trend. On calm, clear nights a nip of frost may settle in cold pockets. Mornings often reveal fields matted with white patches of tiny crystals shimmering and dissolving in the first rays of sunrise. Gardeners cover their fragile crops overnight and uncover them during the day to squeeze out the last few remaining growing hours.

Not all the days are clear and bright. Sometimes rain brings a dreary overcast, obscuring the mountains under a cloak of clouds. Raw dampness invades the valley floors, its chilling bite penetrating forest and field. Merged in a muted gray sea, the foliage quakes in the transition that signals the exodus of autumn. Soon a north wind ushers in the first hint of winter, and in its wake the leaves cling precariously to the trees.

On such a day in mid-October I watched a drenching downpour from my home near the Adirondacks' eastern fringe. Only a few degrees made the narrow margin between raindrops and snowflakes. I was sure the storm was dumping the season's first snowfall on higher summits; in the morning I might be able to photograph some unusual scenes showing a rare combination of fall foliage and snow.

During the night a cold front moved through, pushing out all but a few lingering clouds. In the dark hours before dawn I drove for about thirty minutes to the junction of a trail that leads up one of the higher peaks. I stuffed my heavy winter parka into a pack loaded with camera gear, and with flashlight in hand, began to trot up the trail. Within the first few yards my expectations were realized. Trees heavily laden with wet snow drooped in all directions. The trail was a maze of tunnels formed by arched branches crusted with white frosting.

The subtle light of dawn slowly filtered through the tangle as I made my way up the steep trail. The forest was alive with sounds of creaking trees laboring under the strain of a heavy weight. The branches are barren in winter, but at this time of year the lingering foliage had provided added surface for accumulating snow. A pale glint of light appeared through an opening in the trail. I stepped out on ledges where a sweeping wall of frosty mountains towered before me, etched against the black sky. Their icy summit caps glowed with a rosy tint that blended to deep purple, cascading into ravines and flowing toward the valley floors where the darkness of night still lingered.

Experience had taught me that morning light increases rapidly, so I hastened up the trail in order to be on top for the first rays of sunrise. Ledges and rocks along the path became steeper, and a coating of ice under the snow made treacherous footing that sometimes sent me sprawling. The trail, ducking in and out among scrub trees, offered tantalizing glimpses of surrounding mountains that glowed more radiantly each moment.

Breathlessly I trudged onto the snowy summit ledges just as the sun burst from the horizon. Like the beam of a gigantic searchlight, its shaft pierced under scudding black clouds, illuminating a panorama of dazzling beauty. Stark white summits blended into vibrant red foliage stippled with dark daggers of spruce and balsam. The evergreen boughs were outlined with a dusting of white, creating an illusion of paper cutouts. Ravines were accentuated by deep reds and yellows draining downward into mats of wine-tinted hues in the valleys far below. Colors intensified with every second as the sun climbed higher and flickered in and out among fragments of clouds. Darting shadows cast by the clouds skipped along ridges and icy pinnacles.

It was a magic moment reserved for me alone. I was the only human visitor on this remote outpost, witness to one of Nature's greatest spectacles. Everywhere I turned, beauty was there to be photographed. It would not have made any difference what kind of camera I had; the cheapest or the most sophisticated would have recorded the same fantastic scenery. It was merely a matter of being there at the right moment. And that is one of the special privileges of living in the Adirondacks—being able to experience each day's new beauty and excitement—my home is a threshold to ever-changing enchantment.

Wind began to buffet my summit perch, and I was thankful I'd thought to bring a warm parka. October seemed long gone as I huddled behind a boulder for protection. Plumes of snow swirled out in space and twisted up in the air—miniature tornadoes spiraling all around the ridges. It was barely eight o'clock, but I was content to have experienced more than a day's excitement on top. With an icy wind beating me in the face, I made a hasty retreat off the mountain. A little after nine I was at the bottom again, back to calm and quiet—where it was still October.

Even though the morning had just begun, I knew the special beauty of snow and foliage would disappear rapidly. Leaves curl up in a matter of hours in a cold snap; wind blows the snow off and often a good deal of the foliage as well.

From the valley floor, through a framework of brilliant maples and birches, I got glimpses of surrounding mountains. Their icy summits seemed to beckon, and I felt frustrated because I couldn't be in enough places at once to capture all this grandeur on film. If only I could get up higher, I thought, to someplace where I could see all of it—perhaps from a plane!

I knew of a small airport at nearby Lake Placid village, so I drove to it. The tiny airstrip bustles with activity in summer, mostly that of tourists who come for scenic flights, but in recent years it has also become a home for soaring enthusiasts. Soaring is an exciting sport that takes advantage of the Adirondacks' invisible energies—the atmospheric waves and thermals. A glider can coil upward on these air currents and sometimes stay aloft for hours, just drifting over the corrugated ridges and peaks like a hawk on silent wings.

As I stepped from my car and looked up, a sleek silver glider silently made its approach to the runway. Several more were in the distance, spiraling in slow motion, rising upward on currents that carried them high over the snow-capped peaks.

I checked in at the airport. At lift-off, it was ten o'clock. Two hours earlier I had stood on the summit of a high peak. Now, as we gradually gained altitude, I looked down on magnificent mountain peaks stretched as far as the eye could see—a collection of ice-coated islands in a golden ocean of foliage.

The village sprawled out below, hugging the shores of Mirrow Lake and scattering off toward the larger body of Lake Placid itself. Towering to the north was a single sentinel—the colossal pyramid of Whiteface Mountain. I could see the tiny white cylindrical structure of the Atmospheric Sciences Research Center Weather Observatory balanced on its top. This remote outpost is a facility of the State University of New York.

Our plane winged westward, out over the village of Saranac Lake, located among a cluster of small ponds and lakes radiating in all directions. Saranac, the largest, horseshoes west, then north, toward a multitude of other lakes and a labyrinth of waterways. The plane dipped southwest, approaching the series of lakes dominated by the long arm of Tupper Lake. Flying at 5000 feet, we could see the lakes spreading out endlessly, gleaming like blue jewels in a mosaic of reds, yellows, and greens. There was no snow except for a trace on Mount Morris, where Big Tupper Ski Area reaches up its northern flank.

Turning south, we began the big circle that would bring us back to Placid. Far below, the slender form of Long Lake was stretched out in an open strip for many miles. Attached at each end to a twisting channel called the Raquette River, the narrow sliver of the lake is spanned about midway by a steel bridge where a small village clusters. Where it leaves the lake to flow north in a serpentine course, the Raquette passes through a number of other lakes, including Tupper, and finally leaves the Adirondack Park just before reaching Potsdam. The Raquette is a major tributary of the Adirondack watershed, and its journey continues on to the St. Lawrence.

Still flying south, we approached Blue Mountain, its hulking mass lifting high above Blue Mountain Lake. In a commanding spot just above the lake, the neat little complex of buildings of the Adirondack Museum was visible.

We banked toward the east and passed over Indian Lake, then on toward the tiny settlement of North Creek, where I could see the Hudson flowing by the town. Once a vital artery for pulpwood drives, the river here is now the scene of one of the country's greatest whitewater derbies. As the Hudson gushes bank-full about the beginning of May each year, thousands of spectators crowd into the villages of North River, North Creek, and Riparius to watch the slalom and downriver races. The derby has replaced pulpwood as a local industry, and the expanding recreational use of the river has brought new hope to the communities along its banks.

We made our last turn, going due north, and the pilot brought the plane up to 7000 feet to pass back over the High Peaks. In the distance I could see their little white caps clustered together like a handful of mushrooms, but their expanse gradually spread outward as we approached. The magnificent cone of Mount Marcy stood above all the others trailing out around it in long ranges and isolated groups. The sun had reached its peak, and the colors of autumn folded into the valleys and ravines were dazzling indeed.

The plane dropped a little, and I looked right over the many-toothed summits of the Great Range. At its far end I could make out a tiny pinnacle, still encased in ice and frost—the place where I had stood earlier that morning.

We began the gliding descent toward Lake Placid, and I took one last look east toward the notch between Cascade and Pitchoff Mountains, where slender Cascade Lake lies squeezed between precipitous walls. As the plane settled down on the airstrip again, I checked my watch. Not quite noon. I felt I had lived a lifetime in scarcely half a day, and still had another half day to go home and harvest my garden. The first snow on the mountains was a poignant reminder that I must say farewell to fall.

62

The Plates

1 White birches at Chapel Pond.
2 Morning in an Adirondack meadow.
3 Lapland rosebay (*Rhododendron lapponicum*) thrives only above timberline.
4 Diapensia (*Diapensia lapponicum*) is a tiny alpine plant with blossoms about the size of a dime.
5 Woodland ferns after a rainstorm.
6 Dewdrops reflect the images of spruce needles.
7 A spider guards the center of his domain.
8 Clear water cascades down a rocky stream bed.
9 Spring runoff down the Ausable River.
10 Rainbow Falls plunges 150 feet to the rocks below.
11 A canoeist challenges the rapids of the upper Hudson.
12 At Riparius canoeists swamp during the Hudson River Derby.
13 Mallard ducklings.
14 Rainbow trout.
15 Fly-fishing in the Ausable River.
16 Ruffed grouse.
17 Bittern.
18 Cautious white-tailed deer feeding in a meadow.
19 Rainbow at Connery Pond, near Lake Placid village.
20 Bluebells (*Campanula rotundifolia*).
21 Bloodroot.
22 Rock jutting from the cliff cleaves Avalanche Falls into two streams, one flowing out into the Hudson drainage system and the other through the St. Lawrence watershed.
23 Daisies at Tupper Lake.
24 Immature red-tailed hawk.
25 Porcupine.
26 Chipmunk.
27 Red foxes.
28 Aerial view of Lake Placid village and Whiteface Mountain.
29 Brant Lake village.
30 Sailboats at Essex, on Lake Champlain.

31 Antique steamboats on Lake George.
32 Family fishing from a canoe on St. Regis Pond.
33 Sailing an Idem on St. Regis Lake.
34 Rock-climbing above Chapel Pond.
35 Hikers descend Noonmark against a background of the Great Range.
36 Bear Pond.
37 Little Long Pond in the St. Regis region.
38 Maples and birches in autumn.
39 Snow-mantled maple leaves.
40 Mountain maple leaves outlined by frost.
41 Frost-covered blackberry brier.
42 View of the Great Range from Noonmark after an early autumn snowstorm.
43 Main building of the Ausable Club at St. Hubert's.
44 Hardwoods mingle with snow-dusted evergreens to form a colorful natural tapestry.
45 Canada geese in flight.
46 Mount Marcy viewed from timberline on Algonquin.
47 Skaters at Connery Pond.
48 Ice-cutting, Cascade Lakes.
49 Sleigh, Lake Placid.
50 Snow-laden lean-to.
51 Farm near Wadhams.
52 Aerial view of the high peaks, with Haystack in the foreground and Mount Marcy to left of center.
53 Winter mountaineer on Algonquin looks toward Iroquois Mountain.
54 Aerial view of MacIntyre Range. The prominent summit is Algonquin.
55 Winter mountaineers cross Elk Lake, with McComb Mountain in the background.
56 View of Cascade from Pitchoff.
57 Skier on Whiteface Mountain.
58 The summit of Whiteface in midwinter.
59 Snow-covered evergreens near timberline.
60 Ice-encrusted scrub birch at timberline.
61 The stems of a small plant provide a framework for nature's ice sculpture.
62 Ice-coated blueberry twigs.
63 The top of a ten-foot balsam shows above eight feet of snow.
64 Icicle suspended from a spruce branch.
65 Cascade Lake.
66 Sunset shining through ice-coated birches near the summit of Cascade.
67 Weather observatory on the summit of Whiteface Mountain.

3

4

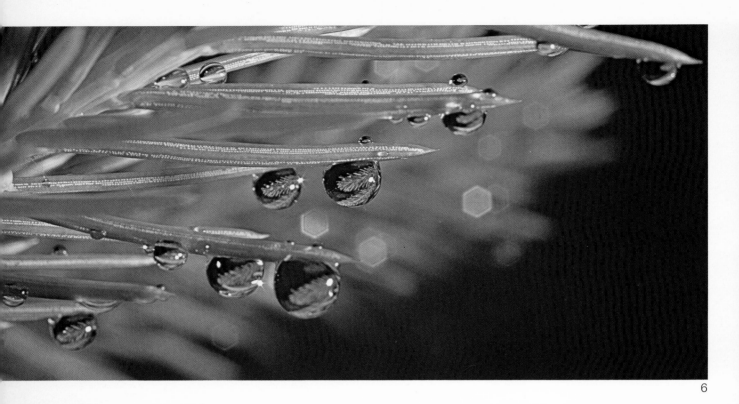

6

7

8

10

11

12

13

14

15

16

17

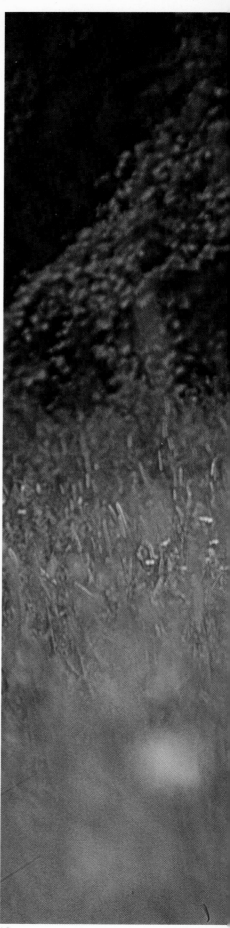

18

24

25

26

27

29   30

31

33

32

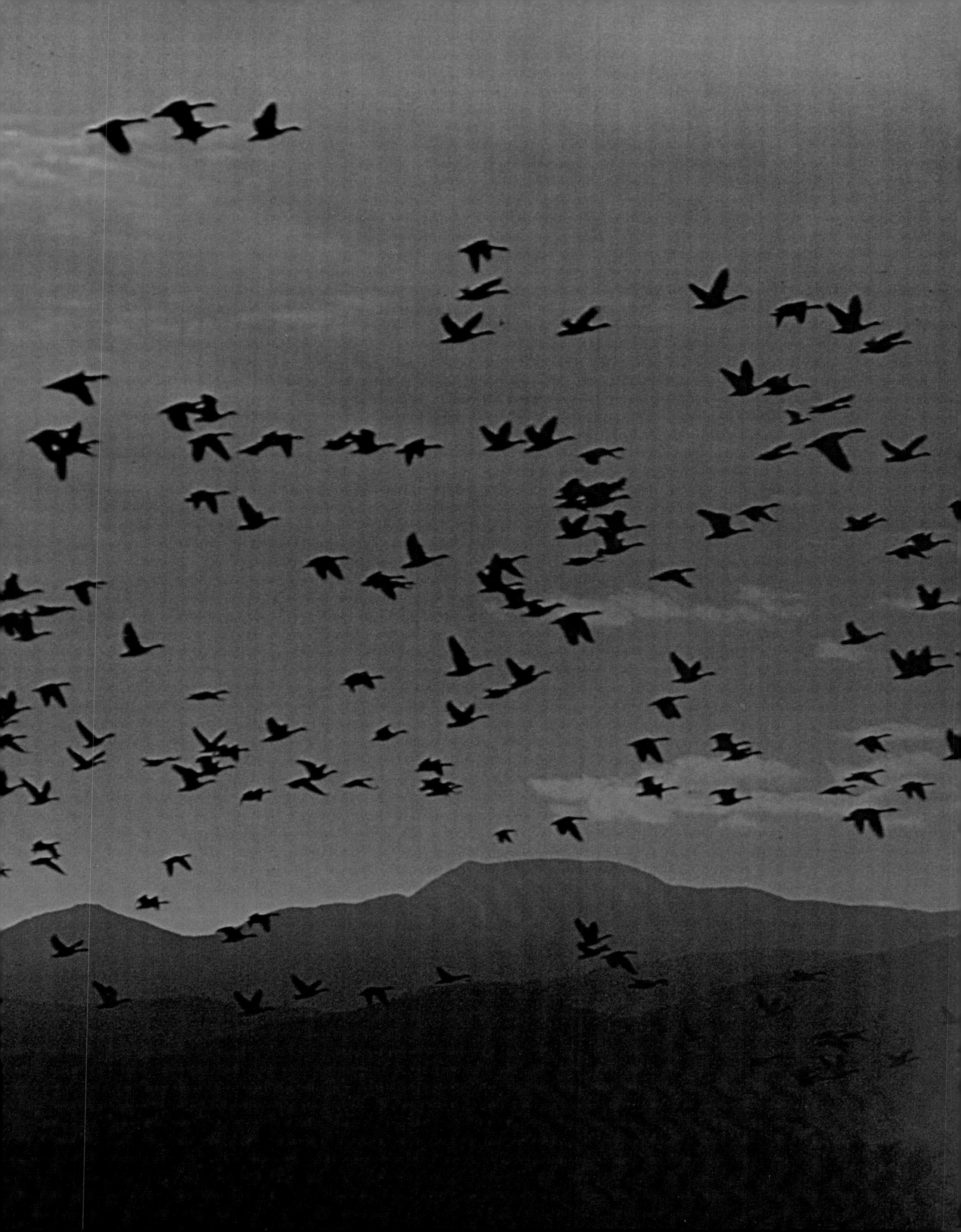

51

55

54   56